William Macintosh

Analytical Review of Twelve Sermons

William Macintosh

Analytical Review of Twelve Sermons

ISBN/EAN: 9783337107413

Printed in Europe, USA, Canada, Australia, Japan

Cover: Foto ©Lupo / pixelio.de

More available books at **www.hansebooks.com**

ANALYTICAL REVIEW

OF

TWELVE SERMONS,

COMPOUNDED OF RABBINICAL ORTHODOXY AND
RATIONALISTIC ABERRATION:
THE OTHER INGREDIENTS BEING SUPPLIED FROM
THE ANIMUS OF THE COMPOUNDER,

AN ORTHODOX RABBI.

"TO THE LAW AND TO THE TESTIMONY: FOR IF THEY SPEAK NOT
ACCORDING TO THIS WORD, THERE IS NO LIGHT IN THEM."

אַל־תּוֹכַח לֵץ פֶּן־יִשְׂנָאֶךָּ הוֹכַח לְחָכָם וְיֶאֱהָבֶךָּ:
תֵּן לְחָכָם וְיֶחְכַּם עוֹד הוֹדַע לְצַדִּיק וְיוֹסֶף לֶקַח:

LONDON:
WILLIAM MACINTOSH, 24, PATERNOSTER ROW.
—
1870.

A. J. LEV,
HEXAGLOT BIBLE OFFICE,
PATERNOSTER ROW, E.C.

THAT the Twelve Discourses announced as a Defence of Judaism are, strictly speaking, only a defence of Rabbinical orthodoxy, there can be no doubt. Many who have discarded that accretion on the pure primitive faith, and many who think worthily in spite of it, can neither feel satisfied with the mishandling of Scripture testimony or of the original words in which Moses and the prophets have conveyed it.

In his Preface, the Rabbi plainly enough states to what armoury he owes his weapons and ammunition. He says: "They have been culled, in the main, from the writings of the principal commentators on the Bible and of our religious philosophers. I have also derived considerable assistance from the controversial works bearing upon the subject, such as by R. Isaac Troki,—by R. Lippman Mühlhausen,—and by R. Isaac Lopez."

ANALYTICAL REVIEW.

PRELIMINARY REMARKS.

THE faithful Custodians of Holy Scripture can have but one desire, that of preserving and holding *intact* the integrity of the high trust and responsibility committed to their charge. To them, therefore, no apology is necessary for such animadversions as the outspoken *infraction* of that integrity have called forth.

That the Sermons* under review are at once an infraction of the inviolable testimony, and the original terms employed by Moses and the prophets in recording it, cannot be denied. Alas! instead of eradicating the old malady, Time seems rather to have rendered it *chronic*, for still the grievous declaration holds good, "The leaders of My people *cause them to err*, and they that are led of them are destroyed." From the way of Wisdom, and from the pure ancestral Faith they are still *misled*. They have been so long accustomed to the spurious issue accredited by Rabbinical orthodoxy, that *essential* standard value—*that* which is the test of their allegiance, that which their Sovereign demands as the *tribute* due to HIS NAME— they have ceased to render. Nay, those who depart from this evil become strange to their own household. No longer accounted as Jews belonging to the fold of orthodox Judaism, they are treated as the illustrious of their race have ever been, by persecuting intolerance. Knowledge of the Will and Word of the Most High must be searched out as hid treasure, otherwise it will not be found. Hence the

---

* A Course of Sermons on the Biblical Passages adduced by Christian Theologians in support of their Faith. Preached in the Bayswater Synagogue, by Hermann Adler, Ph.D., Minister of the Congregation.

declaration: "My people perish for lack of knowledge." The Divine Word, which is not only the higher inner life of man, but the heavenly aliment vouchsafed for the sustenance and growth of that life, has ceased to feed the defrauded and healthless Household, to whom a *leaven*, serving to inflate the head while it corrodes and vitiates the heart—has been substituted for the Bread of Life, the healthful, heart-strengthening stay of "the household of faith." To what, but this pernicious *substitute*, is due *devotional ignorance* and that *superstitious* reverence for lifeless forms and negations, which—while utterly ignorant of the first great command, as an indwelling, rectifying, assimilating and transforming power—relies on the "*shemang*," not only as a present charm, but as a passport to the Divine favour hereafter? Can brambles produce the fruit of the vine? Assuredly not.

That there is *healing* for Israel in the heart-quickening beams of the Sun of righteousness is certain; and many who have felt that salutary warmth have realized its blessedness. Divested of dark age impediments, they ask the way to Zion with their faces thitherward. Free to serve their Heavenly Father in the spirit and life of His first supreme command, they silently operate as rectifying salt, imparting the good that is in them among the inert mass with which they are socially incorporated.

The Reviewer wishes it to be clearly understood that the *very offensive allusions* which accompany the *infractions* complained of are to be considered exceptional, and thus utterly dissociated from the Hebrew community at large. It is simply impossible that the Spanish and Portuguese section, be they orthodox or reformed, could act otherwise than as true gentlemen, incapable of wounding the feelings of others.

The malevolent emotions which characterise some of the descendants of those scattered at the destruction of the Second Temple never found place in that estimable portion of the community, which was happily preserved from the deteriorating influences of a corrupt priesthood and sanhedrin. Having settled in Spain *before* the Second Temple existed, and having never returned from their 2,000 years' sojourn in Spain and Portugal, they have escaped the plague-spot which at times breaks forth in others, that of a *cherished hatred* for the perfect exemplifier of the Father's love in its hitherto unknown degree, "love of enemies." This too often appears, not only in the tone and animus of the communal organ, but of late in the malicious and mendacious diatribes of the unscrupulous N. Meyer.* Why should the Reviewer shrink from the mention of the name which, as if secure of favour and applause, he boldly appends to his calumnies? Perhaps this may help to explain why the writers of excellent articles on various subjects wisely seek to escape not only personal abuse, by adopting *noms des plumes*, but odious liability.

Although none have suffered more cruelly than that section of the people which historically and socially stand so deservedly high in the estimation of those who best know their character, they have always *discriminated* justly between "the workers of iniquity," from whose persecuting intolerance they so grievously suffered, and the righteous exemplifier of the Father's will.

A remarkable instance of this fair dealing we find in a letter to Voltaire, relative to his "Essay on Toleration," by a noble Spanish or Portuguese Israelite: "We hope that the work will be useful not only to Jews but to people in general, in opening the eyes of the several powers of the world; and that it will contribute if not to eradicate, at least to weaken that antipathy and hatred which sinister interests and false policy, rather than the *just* and *pure* tenets of Christianity, keep up in the hearts of men. As you breathe this spirit, sir, you lament the miseries of our nation, whilst you condemn the conduct of some individuals, and the religious errors which have crept into their community. We have been long persuaded that we should always find more protection and humanity among *true* Christians than Deists, notwithstanding their pretended toleration." The allusion here to "some individuals" is a finely pointed irony on this Deist's wholesale mode of maligning the Hebrews. The following extract explains it: "If M. Voltaire had acted according to the principles of sound reason, which he affects to do, he would have begun by distinguishing from the other Jews the Spanish and Portuguese, who have never been mixed up or incorporated with the crowd of the other sons of Jacob. He would have made this *great distinction evident*. I am sensible that it is little

---

* *Jewish Chronicle*, Sept. 23rd, Oct. 21st, 28th. Here the question would naturally occur,—Does this organ represent the mind of the community at large? Can any but accomplices *approve* of thus insulting their neighbours?

known in France, and that the want of proper information on this head has been detrimental on many occasions to the Portuguese at Bordeaux. They are descended in general from the tribe of Judah, and they hold that the chief families settled in Spain from the time of the Babylonish captivity. This is the cause of their distinction, and that elevation of mind observed among them, and which even their brethren of other nations seem to acknowledge. . . . They have preserved purer morals, and have acquired a certain importance, which helps every Christian to distinguish them from the other Jews."

What is now wanted, in the *present chaotic* state of Judaism, is *return* to the truth once delivered. Hence the call, "Return, Israel, unto JEHOVAH thy ELOHIM, for thou hast stumbled by thine iniquity. Take with you words and turn to JEHOVAH, and say unto Him, Take away all our iniquity, and receive us graciously."

SERMON I.

THE First Discourse opens with a sound remark—that of R. Eleazar: "A thorough knowledge of the Law (*i.e.*, Word) would prove a mighty and successful weapon—a sharp sword to cut through the knotted web of sophistry." The Rabbi then proceeds to make manifest how cutting is the action of that Divine weapon, alike on the interventional authority and on the monographic dogma of which he is the defender. Thus he enters the arena of controversy armed with such negatives and negations as his arsenal can supply.

"I was once engaged in such a controversy, when my adversary triumphantly remarked that the *third* word in the Bible proved the truth of the principal dogma of Christianity. The word ELOHIM is there used to denote the Deity, and my antagonist asserted that this word, being in the plural, clearly proved that the Godhead consisted of more than one person. . . . I answered him that the *second* word in the Bible, בָּרָא, refuted his argument." The conclusion at which the Rabbi had arrived was, that the verb being used in the singular, the plural which it governs must be considered singular also.

If, instead of opposing one form of truth to another, the Rabbi had simply stated that the plural noun Elohim denoted "*powers*" distinctively operating in *essential unity*, his antagonist would readily have admitted not only that this Divine unity of LOVE, LIGHT, LIFE, could not have been more emphatically or suggestively embodied in a single word; but that a more inappropriate term than "persons" for invisible powers could not be found. Of this the Rabbi may feel certain, that had *he* wielded the Divine Word, (the sword that cuts two ways,) neither *trini*tarian or *uni*tarian creed—error—could have resisted the mighty power of TRUTH thus made plain to the understanding of those who love Divine Truth more than their creed. Such is the absolutely assertive authority of original forms of speech, that they have only to be *known* to be valued as standard worth. For natural ignorance and creed misunderstanding *direct light is the cure;* to the *healing* beams of that "SUN *of righteousness*" nothing but prejudice is inaccessible.

The inspired historian opens the volume of revealed Truth with בְּרֵאשִׁית, the initial Power, in concrete relation to created beings and things. Now, this initiatory Being (described by a noun feminine) is the Divine Spirit, which at the beginning of time "moved on the face of the הַמָּיִם." The second word to which the Rabbi alludes is בָּרָא, the root of which being בָּר, is identical with דָּבָר, the Word, by whom *Elohim* created all things, visible and invisible. David thus testifies to the Divine Spirit, *i.e.*, Wisdom, חָכְמָה, "By Wisdom hast thou עָשָׂה made, *i.e.*, perfected, them all" (in contradistinction to created). By His Word were all things created (to be perfected). Genesis ii. 3. The fact is, that the things created are by nature (man included) rudimentary, mutable, and temporal; those perfected by the Spirit being perfect and permanent. As the defender of Rabbinical orthodoxy and rationalistic monography, the Rabbi finds it convenient to reduce *Elohim* to a mere idiomatic form of plural, belonging (as he imagines) to "a class of words which, although having the plural form, are to be considered singular." The examples which he has cited in evidence of this mistake belong to a totally different species of terms, the difference being no less than that between essential and relative.

"It is true," continues the champion of orthodoxy, "that the word, (*i.e.*, Elohim,) terminating as it does in ים, has a plural form, but we have as much right on that account to consider it plural as to call the words פָּנִים, 'face,' חַיִּים, 'life,' נְעוּרִים, 'youth,' plurals. ... The term Elohim is of this class of words."

For reasons palpably manifest, the Rabbi *substitutes* our *Anglican singular*, "face," "life," &c., for the *dual* terms of the *original*, thus restricting their highly suggestive forms to their *lowest* sense. In the original, the term פָּנִים at once indicates *superfices* and *interior;* the *outward* (upon which man looks), and the *inner* (which the omniscient eye regards); while in חַיִּים we find not alone *present* but *future* (the "life" which now is, and the "life" to come). In the same manner נְעוּרִים indicates the renewal of youth. It is a grievous mistake to withhold the higher, nobler sense of terms so *manifestly* indicating the true wisdom they thus embody and convey.

The defender goes on to say: "*Elohim* is not the only name applied to *God*." Now here again our Anglican term is at fault; the singular (in the sense of a unit) being "God," the plural is of course "gods" (such as the heathen worshipped before the light of revealed truth had been given to dispel the darkness embodied in either term). Strange, this heathen *misnomer* should be *preferred* by the Rabbi to the original *Elohim*, denoting a unity of Divine powers which no *foreign* term can express! But why should he be so anxious to reduce *that plural* to singular, since we find its own proper singular, *El*, in various forms, as *El Shaddi*, God Almighty; אֵל־שַׁדַּי and אֵל־גִּבּוֹר, mighty God. "There are many others," observes the Rabbi, "that are as strictly singular in form as they are in meaning." Instead of adducing the life-giving name יְהֹוָה always associated with *time*, (past, present, and to come,) with *personality* and with *locality*, the Rabbi substitutes Rabbinical coinage, *i.e.*, *Shem Hamphorish* and *Tetragrammaton*, words of "thundering sound," "clouds without rain." Here the Rabbinical enslavement becomes manifest with allusion to the *interdicted* utterance of that very NAME on which the people are invited, nay urged (at all times and under all circumstances) to CALL. He says: "The sacred *Tetragrammaton*, which, on account of its sanctity, we are not allowed to utter." ! ! "If," continues the Rabbi, "the Deity indeed consists of *more than one Being*, how is it that in Isaiah xliv. 6, we find the word denoting HIM in the plural form Elohim? beside me there is no "*god*." The Reviewer prefers the original Elohim to the Rabbi's foreign designation, which should have been rendered "gods," the allusion here referring to "gods" made with hands, such being *nullities*.

Hitherto the Rabbi has been inculcating on his "congregants" the expediency of *considering* the plural word for essential unity—according to Rabbinical requirements, that is *in the sense of a unit*. Meanwhile this very equivocal ring of moral calibre and quality is not lost on those *without*, who may happen to have a clear perception and just estimate of standard worth. Of his own unsatisfactory mode of dealing, the defender of *orthodoxy* thus speaks: "This *explanation will at once dispose* of the argument sought to be deduced from the expression, 'The Lord said, *We* will make man in *our* image, and after *our* likeness.' Nothing," he adds, "can be clearer than that here the so-called *pluralis excellentiæ* or *pluralis majesticus* is used, and that this form is introduced to give befitting dignity to the narrative of the creation of man, who was formed in the image of the Most High." To support this theory, the Rabbi refers to the use of *our* and *we* in the letter addressed by the Persian monarch to Ezra, as also to the usage of these terms by modern sovereigns.

The Persian usage, we all know, was strictly in conformity with that mode of government, the sovereign acting in *concert with his councillors*, who were deemed so indispensable as to have been designated "*the eyes*" of the sovereign. As regards Anglican sovereignty, it would assuredly be more constitutional, as well as more becoming, to consider the use of *we* and *our* as the expression of a supremacy in strict unison, whether in council or action, with the estates of the realm. To suppose that the use of such pompous and inflated terms is consonant with real dignity is absurd on any occasion, but in that to which the Rabbi refers, it is intolerably so. The Rabbi proceeds to quote a passage rent from its explanatory context: "So God created the man in *His* image," and adds, "as if the Bible would at once dissipate the idea that there could be more than one Deity, the singular form of the pronominal suffix (*i.e.*, his) is used in the very next verse, 'So God created the man in *His* image.'" The Rabbi may rest assured that no one who believes in the doctrine of the Teacher "like unto Moses" can for a moment conceive of more than one Deity; but they do believe that Jehovah, Elohim, is distinctively operative and even indwelling, as love, as life, and as light.

But as the context *explains* in what sense the *created* man resembled his Creator, whose higher union he moreover *prefigured*, (as earthly man could,) why did the Rabbi *separate* the portion that seemed to him favourable to his theory from that, the light of which serves most effectually to dissipate its stifling smoke? In giving the quotation in its entire form, the substituted term of the Rabbi is here replaced by the *original* plural word: "And Elohim created the man in His image, according to His own similitude created He him, *male and female* created He them." Now here דְמוּת plainly implies personality; nor that alone—it denotes *union*, essential and indissoluble. It was not in his *isolated* state, as a unit, that Adam served to represent his Creator in form and mode of being. It was not good for Adam to be alone. As material representative of the higher union, Adam was the fountain which supplied a second self—a dual agency—one in being, twain in person and vocation. Thus did the rudimentary and imperfect man of earth serve to foreshadow the man "Adouni," crowned with glory and honour as the *Reclaimer* of forfeited dominion. It is from him—the Word embodied—that his regenerate עֵדָה is built, (as Eve was from the substance of her earthly lord,) the דָּבָר *by* whom all things were created, and *to* whom (as בַּר) all belong, not only by right of creation but of redemption. He it is who thus speaks: "I will betroth thee unto me for ever; yea, I will betroth thee in righteousness, in judgment, in lovingkindness, and in grace; I will also betroth thee unto me in faithfulness. Thou shalt no more call me Ruler, but אִישִׁי, my *Husband*," (literally, "my man.")

In a careful inspection of the creation of Adam, paying due regard to the terms בָּרָא, to *create*, and עָשָׂה, to *make*, (in our translation,) but properly to perfect from created substance, we shall be able to perceive that, although *ulterior in the order of time*, man *essentially* perfected in the image of the Most High—man inclusive—was first in the *inspired mind* of the narrator, who, in describing the created man, gives *precedence* to the Heavenly, the Adouni, crowned with glory and universal dominion, of whom David, thus foreseeing his glory, speaks: "Adouni, our Adouni, how illustrious is thy Name in *all the earth*,"—then in its *renovated* state, and characterised by righteousness.

The Rabbi, elate in tone, thus proceeds: "One word will suffice to dispose of the argument with reference to the threefold repetition of the word קָדוֹשׁ (holy) in the adoration of the angels."* Having adduced two utterly irrelative texts, he complacently adds: "Were there then three temples? are there three earths?"!!

This text, violently rent from the glorious *subject* and object to whom the adoration is addressed, as also from the *point of time*, (*that* when the *extinction* of evil shall be the crowning triumph of the אֵל־גִּבּוֹר—the Messiah—the culminating glory of rectified humankind, at once the subject and the object to which the glowing seraphim do homage in the thrice repeated "holy" due to His great Name,) serves only to blind the Rabbi, who, owl-like, wants a convenient modicum of light to serve his purpose. The object addressed to the eyes of the prophet in his vision of the remote future, when the whole earth should be filled with His glory, was the ADOUNI, JEHOVAH OF HOSTS. And it was this sight of His enthroned personality that overpowered the holy prophet with a deep sense of unworthiness, thus expressed: "Woe is me, I am undone, for I am a man of impure lips, and dwell among a people of impure lips, for *mine eyes have seen the King Jehovah of Hosts*."

---

* *Seraphim* is the proper term here.

Thus prepared by *self-knowledge* for his high commission, one of the seraphim touched his lips with a *live* coal from off the altar, saying, " This hath touched thee, and now thy impurity is removed." Then, responsive to the question of the enthroned King, " Whom shall *we* send, and who will go for *us ?*" thus perfected and accredited he exclaimed, " **Here am I, send me**." The prophet had just witnessed the object of man's highest, most sublime hope, and on the strength of this vision of future blessedness, he was prepared for his mission, that of *self-sacrifice* and antagonism to the prevailing corruption in doctrine and in practice —but more especially the intense enmity to personality—which characterised those to whom he was sent. The perspective was indeed heart-cheering, but the foreground was repulsive, covered as it was with a tangled growth of evils spontaneous and superinduced. " The prophets prophesied falsely, and the people loved to have it so." The priests *misled*, and their reliant dupes blindly followed those who "caused them to err." The message was to say to priest and people, "Ye hear indeed, but *understand not;* ye see indeed, but *perceive not*," (a state invoking judicial treatment,) hence the command, " *make* the heart of this people *fat*, and *make* their ears *deaf*, and *shut* their eyes; lest they should *hear* with their ears, and *see* with their eyes, and be accessible, that I might heal them." Then said the prophet, " For how long, Adouni?" The answer was, " Until the cities be wasted and empty, and the houses deserted, and the land wholly desolated." Now it is from this state that the people are called to *arise*, in order that, under the *rectifying* power of fresh elements and influences (those *of the Sun of righteousness*), they may be prepared to welcome their King, who comes in the NAME of Jehovah, to bless, to gather, to reclaim, to govern, as foretold.

" Holy Writ," says the defender of orthodox crib and provender, " tells us יְהוָה אֶחָד the Lord, is solely, simply one, and that there are no other ' gods' beside Him—one without any division of parts."

" Holy Writ," and the *Rabbinical accretions* by which its testimony has been so long *overlaid*, are as essentially different as *counterfeit* coinage to STANDARD value—that which Israel's SOVEREIGN demands as the tribute due to His name.

Before putting a few questions to the Rabbi, he must be reminded that in the modern " shemang," " *God*" is substituted for ELOHIM, because it is a *unit;* that being quite as foreign to the original term as "gods" (to any amount known in heathendom), and now the Reviewer would ask, what he means by division of parts as applied to the UNITY of ELOHIM and the BEING of JEHOVAH? He surely is aware that חָד, the root of אֶחָד, is to *unite*, and that א would have sufficed to indicate a unit; whereas unity can only be represented by the original word אֶחָד.

The Rabbi is further aware that יָהּ is equal to the whole of the four-lettered NAME, and that this distinctive form is essential to the glorification of that NAME. For while in His omnipresent Being we all live and move, that same Being has a *personal* and LOCAL *habitation*. If the Rabbi has yet to learn that ADOUNI—a term strictly denoting *personality*—is *interchangeably* used throughout Scripture for JEHOVAH, the sooner he does so the better for himself and those he now blindly misleads. Does he really suppose that there was any "division of parts," or any infringement of unity, when the *Shekinah* appeared in that form suitable to the Divine SPIRIT, and when the Divine NAME was *in* person *that of the Messenger of the Covenant?* Did *these manifestations* at all interfere with the *unity* of *council, design* and *action* of ELOHIM? Is Jehovah, the first and the last, *i.e.*, אֶת, not essentially one because He appears in this dual or combined form? Hence His declaration, "I am the first and—in, or with, the ulterior—I am He."

The Rabbi next quotes the words which the dying patriarch addressed to Judah, and here his own simile, of the foot being clipped for the shoe, fits himself well. The Reviewer must here state that the explanatory כִּי "because," is ignored in our version; and consequently the passage is left to various conjectural explanations. Another passage in which that term properly holds its place may serve to show that it is no less important in the one case than in the other. The passage alluded to is, "The Land shall not be alienated for ever עַד, (כִּי) because the land is Mine." The reclaim of this uniting *hinge* would make the words of the patriarch run thus: "The SCEPTRE shall not depart from *Judah*, nor an administrator from between his feet for ever, כִּי, *because* Shiloh (the peacebringer, the one sent,) shall come; and unto him shall the gathering of the people be." The prophetic eye foresaw at once the dispersion of the flock, and their reclaim to their good Shepherd and fold. The term Shiloh denotes *sent*, " the Father sender, the Son, בַּר, sent to accomplish His good and perfect will, which is, that *all should be saved, and come to the knowledge of the Truth."*

The Rabbi affirms that "throughout the Bible the word Shiloh is never applied to a personage, being the name of a well known town, and 'the place of general and national assemblies.'" The Rabbi here follows his leaders, Rashbam, &c., "The sceptre shall not depart from Judah, nor a lawgiver from between his feet, until he *cometh to Shiloh*, and the people gather to him." Does he mean that the pronoun—because such is his impression—is to be considered the tribe without a head, or that כי may be dispensed with? "I have shown you," he adds, "that the Christian interpretation of the passage cannot by any possibility be correct, opposed as it is to the events of history." Now this is true enough, and simply from this cause, that the term "*until*" gave a wrong idea as to *time* and *season* in the due order of events. Alas! it is only of late that the second coming of the Messiah, "to take unto him His great power and reign," has occupied in the minds of Christians that *primary* and prominent place which it holds in Scripture testimony—a fact which has led many to attribute to the "*suffering*" adrent what really becomes due to that of His "glory," earned through endurance. Let the Rabbi read and consider what is recorded of *Shiloh*, the place which he substitutes for the person: "Go now unto Shiloh, My former place, where I set My Name at the first, and see what *I did to it* for the perversity of My people." He threatens to do the same to the House built for His Name, because of the same perversity, when it should have reached its culminating point of provocation.

SERMON II.

THE defender of orthodox Judaism begins his Second Discourse with a quotation from "the vision of Isaiah, which he *saw* concerning Judah and Jerusalem," an intimation which should teach us to discriminate between the announcement of those future events described in the vision, and the political incidents associated with the immediate reign of the four successive sovereigns under whom the prophet lived and testified and suffered, as a witness to Truth. The vision is preceded by a faithful protest against the retrograde state of his people, serving the Most High with their lips, while their heart was estranged from *His will* and *command*. Hence the complaint: "The steer knows its owner and the ass its master's crib, but Israel doth *not know*, my people doth *not consider*." A bright burst of prophetic light follows; glimpses of the future kingdom of the Man whose name is the Branch, and who shall be called Jehovah, our Righteousness—are caught by those who *do know* and *do consider*. Hence the invitation: "House of Jacob, let us walk in the light of Jehovah."

The Rabbi confines his view entirely to the *foreground* scenery of a landscape, in which there is, for his eye, *no perspective*, no "hope of Israel." To him, alas! the vision is a sealed book.

The reign of Ahaz was that of political agitation and terror. Not only had the confederate chiefs of Syria and Israel threatened invasion, but the appointment of a king for the throne of David of their own selection. Then *Adouni*, the rightful future King of that throne, bids Ahaz ask a sign, in the height or in the depth, for the security of that throne to the house of David. Ahaz, declining thus to try Jehovah, leaves the matter to Him whose counsels of old are faithful and true. Hence the sign given by Adouni himself is that of "the promised seed of the woman," "*the Child born*," "*the Son given*" of the Father, to glorify His law and illustrate its doctrines. However associated with the absorbing interest of local events, the sign given *by the eventual heir of the throne of David* himself, has doubtless a higher import, a deeper significancy, than that of the sign-child or children of the prophet and prophetess, who, if she called *her* child Immanuel, must assuredly have exercised her prophetic faculty in thus characterising him to whom the LAND appertains, (Isaiah viii. 8,) "thy Land, O Immanuel." It was enough that the son of Isaiah and the prophetess served as a sign of the speed of passing events, as his name (verses 3, 4) indicates "speedy booty, hasty spoil." The misconduct of those who occupied the throne was soon to consign it to a vacancy of two millenaries, Zedekiah, a captive in Babylon, having had no successor.

The expression "Jehovah our righteousness," the Rabbi nullifies into a term equally applicable to a city. "This cannot," he adds, "be taken as a proof that the Messiah was to be a Divinity, for the same title is applied to the city of Jerusalem." Now, however such logic may satisfy the Rabbi's disciples, those outside—who own the doctrine of a Heaven-sent Teacher, and are thus taught to perceive and discern between things that differ—firmly believe that when Jerusalem shall have become thus designated, it will be because יְהוֹשֻׁעַ JEHOVAH'S SALVATION *is* THERE. To imagine that, without that good and sufficient reason, any city could deserve to be so called, were worse than foolish.

The next passage to which the Rabbi applies his "verifying faculty," and with no better success, is Isaiah ix. 6, 7. In dealing with his comment no apology is wanted for replacing two important terms, which, in his quotation from our version, he has taken leave to ignore. First then, פֶּלֶא, translated "Wonderful," is properly "Miraculous,"—we may compare it with other passages where the same term indicates the same Being. The term rendered "Counsellor" we find in these reassuring words, "Is thy Counsellor perished?" Truly in Divine counsel, as in unity, there is strength. One of the characteristics of our heavenly mother, Wisdom, is עֵצָה, "*counsel.*" The term אֵל־גִּבּוֹר, rendered "Mighty God," is simply the noun singular of which Elohim is the plural, and therefore we find that very term applied to the personage who changed the name of self-seeking Jacob to truth-glorifying Israel. (Genesis xliv. 24.) And here it may be noted that the form in which the Word appeared has ever been that best suited to the need which required to be met and remedied thereby. אֲבִי־עַד, the "perpetual Father," is frequently alluded to by the inspired writers in reference to the Messiah— שַׂר־שָׁלוֹם, Prince of Peace, the human form with the Divine Word,—whose titles have been enumerated as those due to the Messiah destined to triumph over the father of deception and falsehood, head and instigator of the serpent between whose multiform seed of evil and "the seed of the woman" there must ever exist (Gen. iii. 15) *intense enmity*; the former as legion, embodying evil passions (especially those of the serpentine kind), the latter glorifying the *Word* of *Truth*, that Divine seed implanted in every regenerate heart—thus affiliating man with the Father of lights.

In his habitual practice of undervaluing Truth—essential and relative, where the Messiah's claims or His person are concerned—the Rabbi attempts to show that "Mighty Hero" may be applied to Hezekiah: אֵילֵי מוֹאָב being a term applied to the mighty men of Moab. Now אַיִל is quite a different term, inasmuch as it means not only men of animal power, but horned creatures, the designation אַיִל serving for both the ram and the deer. The original does not imply by כִּי־יֶלֶד יֻלַּד־לָנוּ *i.e.*, to us a child *has* been born. The object of hope being future, the language, like that hope, is spoken of as *present* to the mind of the Spirit, as also to the eye of faith, in the prophet who recorded it. Let us consider if the *negative* goodness, which made that king shine by comparison with the *positive* evildoers who had preceded him, is sufficient to counterbalance his unsubmissive desire of prolonged existence; his *coward dread* of death (through which the everlasting life comes); his *want* of conformity to the Divine will, when told to set his house in order, his appointed time to depart having come; his vanity in the display of his treasures, with the cool indifference with which he heard (as the effect of that ostentatious display) that his sons would become vassals on sufferance of the Assyrian monarch; and finally, with his very low and limited estimate of that "peace and truth" with which he secured the immunity he desired—"in his day." That the predicted grandeur of the Messiah, as Conqueror of death in its most appalling form—in his self-sacrificing mode of securing "Peace" for ever, (as the Prince of Peace,)—of "Truth" for ever, (as the Word of Truth,)—should, by a strange perversity of mind, be applied to the frail mortal, thus as it would seem ironically glorified, is indeed as surprising as it is absurd.

Let us turn from this manifestation of grovelling, tortuous

misapplication, to the glorious promise of the "one master figure, the marvel throughout the ten thousand mysterious characters which are inscribed upon that still unrolling scroll, the same image ever recurs, which, to the eye of faith, makes up the mighty wholeness of the prophetic record."* Truly such jewels require their setting. Of that unapproachable greatness, the prophet whose lips had been touched by a live coal from off the altar exultantly speaks: "To us a child is born; to us a son is given, and his name shall be called Miraculous, Counsellor, the Hero, EL, the Perpetual Father, the Prince of Peace. Of the increase and peace of His government there shall be no end, upon the throne of David, and upon his kingdom, to order and establish it aright. The zeal of Jehovah of hosts will perform this." "How could the title, Prince of Peace," asks the Rabbi, "be applied to Him who Himself said, 'I am not come to send peace, but a sword?'" Has the Rabbi to be told that the WORD —whether in the *human* or the *record form*—is the sharp two-edged sword of the Spirit, "separating between the precious and the base," those who love Truth and those who shrink from its all-manifesting light? Thus has been created a gulf between the ancestral faith—the glorious hope of Israel—which nothing short of the coming of Elijah (to *restore* that pure faith, and to *turn* the alienated hearts of the children to their *forefathers*) can bridge over.

If by the term "Founder of Christianity" is meant that party Christianity dating from Antioch, the Rabbi is "beating the air." True to "the faith once delivered" (and which our Heavenly Teacher reclaimed from the burdensome additions imposed by those who caused the people to err), we believe that the Founder of that faith was the DIVINE WORD *in human form* (as formerly in immaterial substance), nay, *in* that *record*—gorgeously mantled, and devoutly kissed as often as it is brought out of the ark in the synagogue.

"How could 'upon the throne of David, and his kingdom,'" asks the Rabbi, "apply to him who never occupied a throne?"

Is he aware that Jehovah's throne was assigned to His Anointed from earliest time, (Jer. xvii. 12,) David having only occupied it in trust for "HIM *whose right it is*" by every claim, Divine and human. His, as all-creating, all-redeeming, בר—His, as conqueror of death and reclaimer of forfeited dominion—His, as the reward of that hard-

---

* *Hebrew Heroes*, by Bishop WILBERFORCE.

earned service of love. Hence the declaration, "Thy throne, Elohim, is for ever: thy sceptre is a righteous sceptre. Thou hast *loved righteousness* and hated iniquity, therefore ELOHIM, thy Elohim, hath anointed thee with the oil of gladness above thy companions." *Now* the blood-bought right to *save*, to *rectify*, and to *endow*, is his *de jure;* the reward of his soul-travail shall then be realised *de facto*. To whom but the risen Redeemer (whose flesh was incorrupt because sinless) does he allude thus: "Thou hast ascended up on high, thou hast received gifts בָּאָדָם (in the man), yea even for the rebels, that Elohim might dwell amongst *them*." The first bestowal of these spiritual gifts was on the anniversary of the giving of the Law, when thousands, who had only known it as a dead letter, had its first great transforming command written as with a pen of fire upon their hearts; and *that* was but the pledge and earnest of the more abundant shower of blessings foretold by the prophet Joel, and yet due to the same place and people: "Then shall regenerate Israel be among many nations as a dew from Jehovah, that waiteth not for man, nor tarrieth for the sons of men."

"It is asserted," says the Rabbi, "by Christian theologians, that this prophecy (Isa. liii.) refers to their teacher, who, they say, after being persecuted by his contemporaries, offered himself as an atonement on behalf of his nation, obtained for them remission of their sins, and was translated to heaven. The supposed accordance of the events of the Nazarene's life with the prophecy proves nothing." To this conclusion certain rationalistic theorists have helped the Rabbi to arrive; their idea being, that not the eye-witnesses who recorded these facts *at the time*, but casual Greek writers, who lived 300 years after, gave publicity to those then misty traditions, "with a view," he says, "to tally with the prophecies of Isaiah." On equally fallacious grounds he seeks to show why this prophecy could not apply to the subject of the prediction, "because all the chapters from the forty-first speak of a time when Israel would be in captivity. The Nazarene was born while the second temple was still standing, and Israel enjoying comparative independence." Very low must be his idea of independence—*under the Roman yoke, and depending on their sufferance ! !*

The Rabbi seems to suppose that the prophetic utterances kept pace with the political events of that period. To disabuse his mind on that point he has only to refer to the fourth chapter, which contains a prediction of the remote future, when, in proof of Israel's regeneration, the SCHEKINAH shall reappear on Mount Zion as a consuming "fire," and a protecting "cloud," "for upon all the glory shall be a defence;" and in the first chapter he will find the *curses* which procured national dismemberment and (these having attained their culminating point) expatriation. The Rabbi thus proceeds: "'Behold my servant shall prosper' is not once distinctively applied to the future Redeemer, and if this expression is intended to denote the Nazarene, who is believed to be God, how can he be called the servant of God?" Does one who professes to *teach* require to be taught the first lesson given by Moses, in the first page of revealed Truth, which is, that the plural noun Elohim includes the Father and Son, one in BEING, distinctive in *relative* manifestation? It is the privilege of the Son to obey (*i.e.*, serve) his Heavenly Father, in the true spirit of sonship, love—this it was which made self-sacrifice easy and welcome. Far otherwise is it with the *self*-seeking Pharisee, whose service is for reward, or that of the enslaved mind, who dreads punishment. Both must continue to doze, dream, or act in the delirium of false stimuli, until, under the direct light of the Word, they are made free* to think and act aright.

Let us recur again to the primer of Wisdom's school. אֵל, EL is the singular, ELOHIM is the plural, and these are one in essence. Again *Yah* יָהּ is the *future* tense of the verb "to be," thus serving to indicate that JEHOVAH is אֶחָד and his NAME אֶחָד, in other words, Jehovah He is Elohim. Hence it is that the distinction implied, in the title Father and Son, is only *relative*. The Father of lights is invisible and omnipresent; the *Son, who makes manifest the Father's love, is visible and local*, Elohim denoting invisible powers; *El*, the singular noun, visible presence. Hence it was that *El Shadi* conversed with Abraham *face to face, as a man with his friend*, as also with Jacob, when he changed his name to Israel (implying *regeneration*). The Father *sends*, the Son is sent; the Father *wills and commands*, the Son obeys and represents. "We learn," continues the Rabbi, "that these events (*i.e.*, to be 'exalted' and 'extolled,' and that kings should

---

* "He is a free man whom the truth makes free;
And all are slaves beside."—COWPER's *Task*.

keep silent in his presence) were to take place in his life." Let this mistake be corrected at once. It was after he had made his soul an offering for transgression that he received gifts for bestowal; but the prophet especially alluded to the time when, as a Sovereign and Priest, he should subdue all his enemies by the irresistible power of a love which no ingratitude could chill. "Instead of being magnified," says the Rabbi, "he was condemned to an ignominious death." The Rabbi must be reminded that *ignominy belongs to guilt*, not to transcendent greatness. The violent death to which Socrates was condemned by his contemporaries entailed ignominy on them—on him fame. To the Holy One of Israel (devoted to the Father's good and perfect will) no kind or degree of ignominy could have been too excessive. Nothing that men, under the influence of the adversary, שָׂטָן, did, could turn him from his determinate purpose, which was to glorify his Father's will, *i.e.*, "that all should be saved and come to the knowledge of the truth." Thus did he achieve the victory over death, that power which transgression had armed with an awful warrant to have and to hold. Thus did he earn righteously the reward of his soul-travail, that of drawing all men to Him as the Liberator from death's dominion.

The Rabbi having settled in his own mind that not "the Holy One of Israel," but the unregenerate nation is the righteous servant alluded to by the prophet, consistently with this wild notion, concludes that the exaltation and reward were to be during the life-time of those still under the dominion of this greatest, and to them most cruelly disastrous world-monarchy—a low estimate of "elevation."!! He goes on to quote "he shall see his seed," and adds: "This signifies that the servant of the Lord will have an offspring. The Nazarene however is said to have died childless. The term זֶרַע," he adds, "is nowhere used in a metaphorical sense, *it has never any other meaning than natural offspring.*" Has the Rabbi yet to learn that neither the promised "*seed* זֶרַע of the woman" or the embodied seed of the serpent, are *natural* offspring, the former being the Divine Word embodied in *woman's substance*, while the latter is the multiform product of the adversary, characterised as they are by affinity to the father of deceit, fraud, and every evil or venomous characteristic. Hence those only who can truly claim affiliation to the Father of light are "*wholly a right seed,*" a seed to serve the אֶל־שַׁדַּי of Abraham while sun and moon endure. Now it is this seed, the product of the Divine Word, that the Messiah shall see as the reward of his soul-travail, and be satisfied; hence the declaration, "Instead of thy forefathers shall be *thy children*, whom thou mayest make princes in all the earth." Hence also his joyful presentation of the firstfruits of the first resurrection: " Here am I, and the children thou hast given me." His own words uttered in prayer while yet on earth, are: "Those whom thou gavest to me I have kept in Thy NAME; Thine they were, and to me Thou gavest them." The defender of orthodoxy, quoting the words " he shall prolong his days," adds, " This expression in Hebrew is *only applicable to temporal life*"—a miserable unscholarly blunder (as already shown) and one which the assertive חַיִּים should correct, comprising as it does in its *dual* form not only temporal existence here, but eternal life hereafter. To this higher, nobler, enduring state of being, Abraham and the other heirs of promise looked forward as the goal of their faith, well content to be as strangers and pilgrims in the Land covenanted and blood-sealed for an everlasting possession. Well, alas! might the prophet ask, " By whom shall Jacob arise, for he is small?" low in faith and in moral stature. When shall grovelling, self-seeking Jacob become the Truth-glorifying Israel? It will come to pass, but when and how? Must this change await the coming of Elijah? can *prayer* not succeed in the case of individuals? קוֹל יַעֲקֹב is still prevailing, when from the heart. "Now," persists the defender of orthodoxy, "can temporal days be held to refer to his Divinity? for length of days cannot be attributed to God—to *Him* who is the *first* and the *last*." Surely he forgets that these very terms imply a dual relation in the form of אֵת. For as truly as the Divine Being had no beginning or ending, His personal relation to time, and place, and man, is that with which we have to do, and for the knowledge of which we are responsible. It is with His local administration that *Israel* above all has had, and *will yet have to do*. Why should the Rabbi grope at noonday, as in the night, on this all-important subject? He goes on to quote, "I will divide him a portion with the great, and divide the spoil with the strong."—"This clearly refers," says the Rabbi, "to *temporal* triumphs." Here the Rabbi is thinking of *his national view* of the matter. Can *that* be in relation to Parliamentary power and Stock Exchange triumphs, for no doubt *these are temporal alike in their nature and destination!!* The Rabbi would fain find in the relative term לָמוֹ "they," a ground for concluding that not an individual is alluded to, but collective Israel. "This would," says he, "seem to point to a *collective body*." How then would he apply these words: "For the transgression of *my people* were THEY smitten." If the nation is the smitten Redeemer, who are those called "*my people?*" surely not the unregenerate nations of the world. We shall relieve the Rabbi from either horn of his dilemma, not by dogmatical assertion, but simply by referring him to three several Scripture attestations, of *how* the term לָמוֹ is to be applied. The duality implied in אֵת *first* and *last*, is plainly expressed in the relative plural pronoun "them," in the following passage from Zachariah's prophecy: "He shall be a Priest upon his throne, and the counsel of peace shall be between '*them*.'" Again we find the sovereign appropriating as insults to himself such as are offered to his personal representative. The irony is intense, the rebuke is withering. "So they (*i.e.*, the priests in the Temple) estimated MY value at thirty pieces of silver, and Jehovah said unto me, cast it to the potter, the notable price at which I was valued by them . . So I took the thirty pieces of silver in the house of Jehovah, and cast them to the potter." Again, "They shall look upon ME whom they have pierced, and mourn over HIM as one mourneth over an 'only son,' and be in bitterness for HIM as one is in bitterness for a 'first-born.'" The Sovereign was insulted in the person of his ambassador and representative, the Father in that of his only son, his בְּכוֹר; hence the proper application of the plural terms, "we," "they," "them," in relation to the Divine unity, thus unmistakeably indicated by pronouns used interchangeably. "Made *intercession* for the transgressors." "To whom could the Nazarene pray?" asks the Rabbi, "seeing that he was said to be God himself."

What does Scripture tell us? "And Jehovah saw that there was no man, and wondered that there was no intercessor, therefore *his own arm brought* salvation, His righteousness sustained Him*. Priests there were, but they neither interceded for themselves or others. Prophets there were, but they deluded the people, seeking to please them with plausible flatteries; saying peace and security, when on the brink of the culminating evil which caused their exile and dismemberment. Well is it for us all, that our

---

* יהשוע in Greek guise, *Jesus*, in Hebrew, JOSHUAH.

Supreme Priest *ever lives to make intercession,* and that to the uttermost bound of time, for up to that point will it be required. The Rabbi winds up this discourse by stating that his arguments have been chiefly supplied from rationalistic celebrities, namely, Gesenius, Hitzic and Knobel, all of whom considered the law and the testimony as obsolete, and therefore useless. The Rabbi considers their commentaries on Isaiah *classical;* they may well therefore rank with the *Greek mythology,* and occupy a place on the same shelf with the sermons whose pages they have served too manifestly to characterise.

SERMON III.

In his next Discourse the travesty of the inspired prophet's testimony concerning the Messiah's suffering advent is complete. He begins by "an *analysis* of some of the expressions to prove that the interpretation of Christian theologians could not be the true one."

It is now the doctrine of "*vicarious* atonement" that he seeks to nullify, forgetful that he would require first to overthrow the whole Levitical economy, which he may be assured has only been *suspended* during the present interregnum of the Theocratic administration. For as surely as the morning and evening sacrifice *prospectively* pointed to the "Holy One of Israel" (whose blood did *cover* מְכַפֵּר the sins of mankind), so surely shall the renewal of that offering point *retrospectively* to the same peace-speaking blood of the Lamb of Elohim, provided (as His remedial means), and that before the commission of the first transgression, in which have been implicated the innocent and guilty—in which the very* אֲדָמָה from which man אָדָם was created, was implicated—its *spontaneous* product, like that of man's unregenerate nature, having ever since been worthless as negative; and even noxious as positive. The poisonous bite of that intellectual tool made use of by the father of lies was indeed mortal in its effects; but the antidote provided (*i.e.*, the Divine Word in human form) was destined to bruise under His heel the serpent's head. Hence the declaration, "Look unto Me and be saved, all the ends of the earth, for I am Elohim, none other."

We know that *rationalistic theorists*, from Maimonides down, have, on the warrant of their philosophical monography and their law of *evolution*, treated these solemn truths (appealing as they do to our eyesight and consciousness) as myths and fables, insomuch that whatever in the record of inspiration interfered with their own

---

* "Ground."

shallow and purblind notions and theories, was "explained away;" their "verifying faculty" thus stripping Scripture testimony of all soundness, substance, and vitality.

"How monstrous a doctrine," continues the Rabbi, "how repugnant to all that the Bible tell us of the righteousness of God, that an innocent, sinless man should suffer punishment which the guilty have entailed upon themselves." The Rabbi, declining to enter on "the question of hereditary sin," says, "Let us consider the assumption which this statement (*i.e., vicarious atonement*) involves, that God by himself is unable to forgive sins."!!

Has he forgotten what was said to Moses, "Let them beware how they provoke *him*, MY NAME is *in* him (*i.e*, His personal messenger), and will not forgive." The *incorporeal* form then enshrining the Divine Being could not atone, could not pardon:—only the Holy One of Israel, woman-born, could thus magnify the righteous law yet clear the guilty, making them as His lawfully reclaimed purchase, His own, the reclaimed jewels of His many crowns. Those who have turned many to righteousness—as the reclaimed gift of the Redeemer—shall rise to honour; others to shame, contempt, and bitter self-reproach. (Daniel xii. 2.) *Here* we have the WORD. If we reject it as *Light*, we invoke its condemnation now, and its inquisition hereafter as FIRE. "Is not my Word a Fire?" saith Jehovah. The grace of our Redeemer does *not* release us (as the Rabbi erroneously assumes) from our *individual responsibility*, gratitude for that unmerited gift proving an infinitely more constraining motive for heart-loyalty, than either hope of reward for heartless service, or dread of punishment for neglected duty.

"No one can," persists the Rabbi, "no one need make expiation for our sins. *We have no mediator to save us from the effects of our guilt, but our own repentance*, by which we hope to obtain the forgiveness of our God. *We require nothing but our own repentance.*" David knew better; not only did he *sincerely repent*, he moreover earnestly prayed for a "*new heart and a right spirit.*" "Cleanse thou me from secret offence and presumptuous sins." "Sprinkle me with hyssop." The blood sprinkling not only prepared the high priest for entering into the holy of holies, but was required for the book of the law, the altar, the officiating priest, and all consecrated things. The destroying Messenger of old looked upon the blood sprinkled thresholds and door posts, *that*, not the questionable repentance of those in the dwellings, arrested his destroying agency. The Lord looked upon the blood and respected the dwellers because of His own appointed sign and pledge of salvation, for which repentance and gratitude (ever as effect follows cause) became due. "The atonement of the priest," says the Rabbi, "was of no avail unless he afflicted his soul, and passed the day in solemn repentance and sincere contrition for his iniquities." Our Supreme High Priest (after the order of Melchisedec) has the peculiarity of being "holy, harmless, and *separate* from sin—a true Nazarene."

The Rabbi next attempts to show, with no better success, that "the effects of unmerited salvation through the vicarious atonement are nugatory. Let us," says he, "now examine what would be the consequences of the existence of vicarious atonement. The good man and the sinner would be reduced to the *same* level." Now it is probable that *his* "sinner" is one who has, by overt acts, entitled himself to that epithet; and that *his* "good man" is one whose outward demeanour, however faultless in the sight of men, may be a mere whited sepulchre in the sight of Him who cannot be deceived—instead of the open misdemeanours of the ignorant criminal, may exist fraud, guile, and other serpentine attributes.

Thus he proceeds: "The righteous man who sinned not, and the sinner, *both alike would receive the Divine grace*—the former by *his own* merit, the latter by *the merit of his Mediator*, and the whole end and purpose of our earthly life would be stultified; and if it were so, should man yield up his pleasures, his passions, his material interests, his self, to good works *that may be dispensed with, to virtues that are not necessary?*"

Can the stultification of the Rabbi be more complete? The idea of gratitude as a *motive* for good works and every virtue has never, it would seem, even dawned on the mind of this curious casuist. Does he suppose that the faith which in Abraham was productive of loyal obedience could have been dispensed with? Did his sacrifice of earthly pleasures, passions, and material interests, for the future inheritance of faith, lessen his present enjoyment? Was this noble end and purpose of his earthly life thus stultified? If we cannot find in *gratitude* (for unmerited salvation) a motive for all that is elevating, noble, and disinterested, we can never rise from very low grounds. "Indeed," he continues, "the theory of mediation, when carried to its extreme consequences, would be a monstrous reversal of the Divine scheme of man's creation and destiny. No! such cannot be the way of the perfect judge. The Pentateuch and the prophets tell us most unequivocally that it is not. . . . ." If the Rabbi acts as their interpreter, this would certainly be the result, for nothing of soundness, substance, utility, or even organic structure would remain. "I have shown you," he goes on to say, "that this chapter cannot refer to the Nazarene acting as mediator of mankind. Let me now submit to you the *true* interpretation of the prophecy. Our expositors agree in saying that the servant of the Lord here spoken of is Israel. 'Thou art my *servant* Israel, in whom I will be glorified.' All the preceding chapters have spoken of the glorious exaltation that awaits Israel." Here the Rabbi requires to be reminded that collective Israel is *invariably* addressed and described by a *feminine* noun: "Therefore I will allure *her* and bring her into the wilderness, and speak comfortingly to *her* . . and *she* shall sing there as in the days of *her* youth, and as in the day when *she* came up from the land of Mizraim. And in that day, saith Jehovah, thou shall call me אִישִׁי, *i.e.*, husband, literally 'man.'" (Hosea ii. 18.)

In what the Rabbi takes leave to call his *true* interpretation, we are required to *reverse* this *grammatical* order and distinction. "He" is to be considered "we;" but should the latter term be used discreditably, as "all *we* like sheep have gone astray, and Jehovah has laid upon *him* the iniquity of all," then it is to be considered the nations. *His* words are: "And *we* (the nations of the earth) esteemed 'him' (the nation) not." The Lord caused "*him*" (the nation) to suffer sorrow for the transgression and iniquity of others!!

Would it not be wiser to own that national transgression and iniquity are the bitter consequences of heart aliency; and that for the sufferings inflicted by "*others*"—whose deeds belied their title and professions—they will be called to a severe reckoning by Him who both taught and illustrated loving-kindness—that which overcomes evil with good. Nay more, that by withholding from the least of His destitute brethren the practical evidence of their love to Him, He will appropriate the neglect as His own; thus will He negative their claims to His favour: "I never knew you, depart from Me, ye workers of iniquity; for inasmuch as ye did it not to these My brethren, ye did it not to Me." (Matt. xxv. 45.)

To follow the tortuous process of the Rabbi would be alike revolting to reason and subversive of Truth; suffice to say, he is quite as remorseless in his treatment of the *structure* of Scripture, as Torquameda was (in the application of his racks and screws) to that of the stray sheep forced into Rome's wolf-fold, there to experience that the tender mercies of the "workers of iniquity" are cruel.

This wonderful sermon closes with the following peroration (only that *"we"* and *"our"* must be considered the nations): "They will say Israel has been wounded for *our* transgressions, bruised for *our* iniquities, the chastisement of *our* peace was upon 'him,' and by 'his' (*i.e.*, the nation's) stripes *we* are healed. We were permitted to afflict him that *our redemption might be effected.*" Scripture tells us that for the indulgence of evil passions against the covenant-people in the day of their calamity, the nations invoke righteous retribution, not, as the Rabbi pretends, redemption!! The Rabbi interprets, "Through his knowledge shall My *righteous* servant *justify* many,"—"bring them to virtue." He does not yet know that this gift of the Spirit, through the Word, does not justify. The LORD's testimony of His perfectly upright servant Job was, that he, as a righteous man, "did good and eschewed evil." But what was this righteous man's own confession? "I have heard of thee with the hearing of the ear; but *now mine eye hath seen thee, therefore I abhor myself, and repent in dust and ashes.*" Then it was that he became worthy to act as *intercessor* for his three mistaken friends, whose reproaches had been so cruelly misdirected.

By way of stilting his lame arguments, the Rabbi, referring to the profound grief of Moses, who offered to make an atonement for that particular sin which demonstrated man's natural proclivity to evil, says: "Did the Lord accept this vicarious atonement? Did He accept this offering of the noble, self-denying hero? Did *He take the life of Moses* the meek, the faithful, and *permit his blood* to be an expiation of the people's sin? No; the Lord rejected his 'vicarious atonement,' . . . and for this reason; that it would have been of no avail. The whole world wanted an atonement, and one worthy of His name. He provided 'one mighty to save.'" The quotation goes on: "He proclaimed, whosoever has sinned against me, him will I blot out of my book." In fact the case is so inappropriate, that the Rabbi must have been reduced to the uttermost farthing to hazard it, even within the walls of his own synagogue. The sacrifice of man, however innocent, could not have saved the sinner; what then becomes of those who wilfully blot themselves out of the book of life? With what body shall they rise? Certainly with that which is the Redeemer's purchase and gift! The Rabbi's standard of greatness is low indeed—that of being "equal to the mightiest of the earth in honour and glory." Has he to learn that the kingdoms of this world and their false glory shall become as the chaff of the threshing floor; and that their political constitutions shall be no more when the kingdom of righteousness and peace shall have superseded them? Looking from the rationalistic point of view, the Rabbi sees development instead of final dissolution for things temporal. He adds: "How sublime is this view of the prophet, looking, as it were, from the summit of his prophetic intelligence." ! !

SERMON IV.

The Rabbi opens his Fourth Lecture by indicating the method by which all arguments of Christian theologians may be refuted.

"1st. Not to trust the rendering of the disputed texts of the Anglican version, for," he adds, " it cannot be denied that its authors were swayed by dogmatic misconceptions." If by " authors "—a most inadmissible term where Scripture is concerned—the Rabbi means translators, the misconceptions he warns his disciples against are but too manifestly due to the Rabbinical orthodoxy. One instance may suffice to show this. Throughout Scripture, wherever the combination of the Divine Being with personality is found—in the prophecy of Ezekiel it occurs 170 times—that combined *Adouni-Jehovah* has been changed into " Lord God," the object having been to ignore this suggestive indication of personality. (In the forthcoming revised version it is devoutly hoped that this flagrant inaccuracy may be rectified.) The Rabbi continues: " Refer to a translation composed by a scholar thoroughly versed in the Hebrew tongue." Now, much as the knowledge of the mere structure is wanted, fidelity to the integrity of the text is of infinitely more importance ; moral honesty being the highest quality of a translator, otherwise there will be attempts to evade, qualify, discolour, or even nullify the most important truths. Hence in translations we find *angel* substituted for אִישׁ (man), as also for אֱלֹהִים * (Elohim). Is this not vitiating the text? and if it cannot be justified, why is it permitted? The Rabbi recommends his congregants, &c., to " turn to the Hebrew," but we fear to little effect,†

---

* Psalm viii. 5.

† " Unto many, many of us it has been a spring shut up—a fountain sealed." " The Torah alone lies neglected, forsaken ; parents provide their children with instruction in numerous languages, but they *except the sacred one*—the language in which God speaks to us. . . We see our children well versed in the knowledge of art and science, skilled in every worldly accomplishment, but they lack . . . the knowledge of God's word."

according to the low estimate to which it has been reduced, and in which it is held at the present time.

"2nd. Do not be satisfied," he continues, "with examining the passage as it stands by itself, but refer carefully to the context." Excellent advice, which the Rabbi is rather apt to forget, thus leading to the inference, that he must have some special reason in his *next illustration* of these rules for thus pressing it; the text to which they are to be applied being thus translated: "The Lord thy God will raise thee up a prophet from the midst of thee, of thy brethren, like unto me, unto him shall ye hearken." The following promise and declaration we have from the mouth of JEHOVAH himself: "They have said well in that which they have asked, I will raise them up a prophet from among their brethren like unto thee: *I will put My words in his mouth, and he shall speak unto them all that I shall command him. And whosoever will not hear the words which he shall speak in My name, I will require it of him.*" The Rabbi having detached from the context this very important sentence, it is here replaced as part of the whole passage.

The Rabbi has previously asserted that plural nouns in Hebrew are frequently to be considered singular; but now that it suits his purpose to reverse the matter, he says, "the singular is often used in the Hebrew for the plural"—a due discrimination between things that differ in the sense of essential and relative, would prevent his confounding these distinctions. The Rabbi admits that נָבִיא means a single prophet; but his theory requires that not a prophet, but succession of teachers should neutralise the text. "In the same chapter we find that diviners who speak their own minds are not to be listened to; the mark of the accredited prophet being that he should speak the words of ELOHIM."

Rabbinical Judaism (in affinity with that rationalism of which Maimonides is the unscrupulous leader and instigator) ignores *mediation* and the need of it; the Rabbi therefore finds himself in a delicate predicament, the promised antitype being mediator, prophet, and leader. The people saw their Elohim on Sinai as "*a consuming fire;*" hence their conviction of the *need of a mediator* to stand between them and consuming holiness—that *fire* which rectifies by assimilation with its element, Divine LOVE—was unapproachable to the perverse and self-centred. Nor will it be otherwise on Mount Zion, where Jehovah shall rectify as silver from inherent and contracted dross, His people; hence the dismay of those who, unconscious that their *merits* are worthless, ignore a mediator. "Sinners in ZION are afraid, terror hath surprised the hypocrites; who can dwell with consuming fire—who of us can dwell with perpetual burning," *i.e.*, the spirit of judgment. Isaiah xxxiii. 14.

The Rabbi, in order to get out of the difficulties of his text, begins by throwing a little dust in the eyes of his disciples. "*What*," he asks, "was the subject of Israel's request? Did they ask for a Redeemer to *save their souls*, or to *give light unto the heathen?* They did not ask for a *mediator to die for their sins*, and to *atone for the original sin of Adam* (!!) but simply *for one or more persons* (human beings) to communicate to them the Divine will. (!!) They asked for a teacher, and a teacher was vouchsafed them." Here the text, curtailed of its vitally important context, is given. "Can this prediction," he asks, "refer to the Nazarene? Could his appearance, 2,000 years later, be a *sufficient reason* that they should not hearken to *diviners in Canaan.*"*!!* "Moses *evidently alludes to a line of prophets*.(!!) None of the prophets were to be divinities, who from their very natures would be exempt from sin and falsehood." When the Rabbi has cast his *interventional* authorities "to the moles and to the bats," he will thankfully accept the fact that the promised prophet, by whose mouth Jehovah's will was shown, combined in his own person the ministries of PROPHET, PRIEST, and KING, anointed as he was by the Holy Spirit.

"Now," says the Rabbi, "I boldly challenge every professor of the Christian faith to tell me where it is stated that the prophet like unto Moses was to declare *a new revelation.*"!! The prophet who spoke the words of Elohim *so separated* the precious of Divine authority from the base—of Rabbinical device—so practically illustrated the doctrine enunciated in the first great commandment, that his teaching and action might well have been *new* to those accustomed to the inflating leaven of the Scribes and Pharisees, by whom the bread of life had been withheld. It was new and startling to hear the prophet like unto Moses speak the words of Elohim in His name— to see him drive out the traffickers from his Father's house of prayer. And what was the scourge? A few cords from עִזִּים, originally given to *remind* them of their *highest* obligation, which had then and there been so shamefully forgotten. Such a demonstration of holy zeal for the sanctity of the Name, thus outraged in the sight of the nations, had been unknown since the prophet Jeremiah testified, and suffered* for his testimony. It was *strange* to speak boldly in defence of Truth, and yet under *personal* wrong to be silent. The characteristic of the Chief Priests, Scribes, and Pharisees who loved the applause of men, and acted from motives inspired by self-love, ambition, and interest, was directly the reverse. So new, so strange was an illustration of Divine greatness, that He who was a Sanctuary† to some, became a stumbling-stone to others, as the prophet foretold. When the Holy One of Israel thus practically vindicated the honour of the holy Name, did the Chief Priests, as official guardians and custodians, offer resistance to the prophet like unto Moses? No; they acted as conscience-stricken cowards, without a word to say in behalf of *their toleration* of the *desecration*. It only intensified their hate, which thus excited, they reserved for a convenient season, practically to manifest in its fury. Hence the prophetic declaration: "*I will make you base and contemptible before all people,*" and so they have continued to this day, "divided in Jacob and scattered in Israel;" but it will not be always so. There shall come a time when their offerings shall be acceptable, as in the day when the covenant of life and peace was made with Levi. The heart of stone shall then have given place to the new heart, on which shall be inscribed holiness and loving obedience.

The Rabbi ventures on a new subject thus: "This verse, which at first sight seems startling to the unwary, is as follows: ' They shall look upon ME whom they have pierced;'" here the Rabbi omits the context, in the words preceding the text and after, *i.e.*, "*I will pour out upon the House of David and upon the dwellers in Jerusalem the spirit of grace and of supplication.*" Then come the words cited, which are followed by "*and shall mourn for him as one mourneth for an only son, and be in bitterness as one is in bitterness for a first-born,* הַבְּכוֹר*.*" These words the Rabbi takes leave to accommodate to his theory, which is, that the great and universal mourning here spoken of (when all the families shall mourn apart and their wives apart) means only for "one who may happen to be 'pierced' in war." He adds, "So great shall be the immunity

---

* Jer. xxvi. 11. † Isaiah viii. 14.

of the children of Israel, they would be surprised and dismayed*— they would look upon it *as a humiliation.*" Here is *bathos* in its extreme. Can paltering with the Divine record go farther?

The Rabbi does not seem to know that the personal *pronouns in their application to the Divine Being are used interchangeably;* the verse selected by him being an instance of this remarkable peculiarity; hence his notion that *the person mourned and wept for, is not identical with* HIM *to whom prayer is addressed.* "The fact," says the Rabbi, "that must weigh with us most strongly is, that the dogma . . . is utterly at variance with the plain teachings of Scripture. It is asserted that Israel shall pray to that God whom they had slain; to that God who assumed the form of man, and offered himself as an atonement for the sins of mankind; to that other portion of the Deity which was not invested with humanity." It is absolutely declared by the inspired prophet, that the spirit of grace and supplication shall *cause the prayer* and the mourning which the Rabbi ridicules. Joseph's brethren, who "despised" him as a *prophet,* and who were totally unconscious of him as a saviour, were eventually constrained by *inner consciousness* of their own perfidy (and his gracious return of good for evil) to loathe themselves and honour him. How magnanimous his re-assuring words: "Be not grieved nor angry with yourselves that ye sold me hither, for ELOHIM did *send me before to preserve life* . . to preserve for you a posterity in the land, and *to save your lives by a great deliverance.*" This is what Moses teaches—will orthodox Sadducees not accept it?

"I ask," says the Rabbi, "can a plurality be attributed to him who has declared himself אֶחָד." Elohim is a plural noun nevertheless. He whose Being is unity, *i.e.*, אֶחָד, is ELOHIM, one and indivisible. Does the Rabbi suppose that יָהּ (yah) is not *identical* in† essence with יְהוָֹה, and that *El* is not essentially identical with

---

* The person who is the occasion of this unprecedented sorrow and supplication is only some one who happened to have been *slain in the war by the invading nations.* Thus he takes leave to twist the text, "They shall look up to me for him they (the nations) have pierced."

† Love, which is the Divine nature, being invisible, must have a personality in which, as a "sanctuary," to make it manifest.

Elohim; alike in the אֶל־גִּבּוֹר who wrestled with Jacob, and the Saviour, אֶל־גִּבּוֹר, who gave his life as world-wide Redeemer.

The declaration, "Thou canst not see my face; no man can see ME and live," was in answer to the request, "I beseech thee, show me *thy glory*," an impossibility in man's mortal body; but His "face" in *human* form had no terror. Abraham, Jacob, Moses, Joshua, Manoah, Gideon, all saw and spoke with ADOUNI-JEHOVAH, face to face.* He quotes a passage, which only goes to prove that HE, with whom Moses spoke, whose similitude was seen by the seventy elders, did not *thus* manifest his *personal* presence to the *unregenerate* multitude, who would forthwith have made some metal or stone image before which (as representative) to bow down; such, indeed, is the reason assigned for *their* having seen no similitude on the occasion referred to.†

---

* Wherever human attributes refer directly to Elohim, in the Hebrew text, the Targums ascribe them to him whom they call the WORD of יְהֹוָה—the glory of Jehovah and the Schekinah. Talmudists continually speak of Elohim as existing in human form, and Maimonides himself, in the very first sentence of the Moreh Nevuchim, says that El Shadi, in human form, was the prevailing opinion when he wrote his book. At the coming of the Messiah (as it is evident from the Targum), and for a thousand years after, as appears from the Zohar, the Talmud, and most Rabbinical writers down to Maimonides, and even after, till *his opinions acquired authority*. It is the universal revelation of Moses and the Prophets to be understood in its grammatical sense as by them recorded. Of this self-entitled authority a Rabbi thus speaks: "Why does he call such an one a heretic, when many greater and wiser than he have walked in this opinion, according to that which they saw in the Scriptures, and still more in the Agadoth, which imply that doctrine?"

† Deut. iv. 15, 16.

SERMON V.

Sermon V. begins thus: "I resume my course of lectures on the Christological passages of the Bible. Great stress," says the Rabbi, "is particularly laid upon the fact that this Psalm (the 2nd) declares in unmistakeable terms that he is the Son of God." We read in the 6th verse, "The Lord hath said to me, Thou art my son, this day have I begotten thee;" and "Kiss the son lest he be angry, and ye perish from the way, when his wrath is kindled but a little." "Now," says the Rabbi, "the first question that should be asked by the intelligent enquirer is—How do you know that these verses apply to your Messiah? We receive no satisfactory answer—dogmatic assertions only are offered. This dogma—that the Nazarene was literally the Son of God—is surely," he adds, "the most monstrous, the most repugnant to reason. (!!) . . . The holy God, whom Holy Writ brings before us as exalted so infinitely high above all imperfections inherent in man's nature, that Supreme Being (I shudder while I say it) is lowered to the level of one of those deities with which the mythology of Greece peopled their Olympus." (!!!) . . . Here the Rabbi seems to have been seized with a paroxysm of mythic declamation. Having subsided, he goes on thus: "How untenable is the assumption that the son here spoken of is like the Father, a portion of the Godhead. 'Ask of me, and I will give you the heathen for your inheritance, and the uttermost parts of the earth for thy possession.' Now, if the Son be a Divinity like the Father, and equal to him, why need he ask that any favour should be granted him? Is he not omnipotent? Is not the whole earth . . . his possession?" The Reviewer will not trouble the Rabbi with either dogmas or assertions, but simply put a few questions which it is impossible for him to answer, until, ceasing to grope in the dark, he shall have come to the light of the Sun of righteousness. By what power did Elohim create all things, if not by his Word or Son, the latter (בָּר) being the root of the former (i.e., דָּבָר), and if Son, why should he not be identical in Being with the Father, although, as the distinctive term "*Son*" implies, relatively subordinate. If the Rabbi admits that by His WORD דָּבָר, ELOHIM created all things visible and invisible, he must necessarily believe that the Divine WORD is omnipotent; while the human form, which enshrines that POWER in a condition which betokens perfect subjection to the FATHER'S will, is told to "ask" and receive, that his joy may be full. This being assuredly a great subject, a small mind, accustomed to a groove, can take in nothing beyond its vicious circle. Abraham believed it, and rejoiced in the belief—hence his faith was counted to him for righteousness. He was no stranger to *Adouni*, the personal King of Israel, whom the prophet Isaiah *saw with his eyes*. Alas! so great is the antipathy of modern orthodoxy to the personality thus described as the Anointed, that had the Rabbi lived in the days of Manassah, he would, in all probability, have justified the sentence he passed on Isaiah for the utterance of this (to his ill-informed mind) *blasphemy;* and would have thought he thus merited the violent death to which he condemned that glorious witness to Truth—a mode of death betokening *severance*** from the orthodox portion of the nation. But Manassah lived bitterly to repent this his crowning atrocity. Through penitent prayer he received the gift of faith and regeneration; the new heart and right spirit were given him, and as a sincere penitent he died. The Rabbi finds no difficulty at all in his own theory, which is, that ELOHIM has *no son* (in the sense of בַּר, creator; or in that of בֵּן, the "son given," to build up the household of faith to the honour and glory of the Father's Name); Israel, collectively, being the son acknowledged by him, however opposed to the fact that Israel, collectively, is *daughter*, or *house* בַּת, *not* בֵּן (son) *i.e., builder*:—so the Rabbi must submit to be set to rights by the assertive force of *original* words thus speaking in defence of Truth. The quotation from Hosea relates to the special son—"the Holy One of Israel."! When He alludes to the *regenerate* people, it is as a "betrothed bride." Such being the endearing title the Anointed gave to His future crown of rejoicing.

"How often," says the Rabbi, "does the Lord call himself our Father. 'Is he not thy Father, hath he not acquired thee.' As a

---

* By the order of Manassah, at the instigation of the priests, Isaiah was sawn asunder.

father he thinks of us, loves us, protects us, cares and provides for us." And what has been the return? *Deviation* from His supreme authority—*evasion* of His direct requirements—the *substitution* of interventional misguidance. Hear His declaration: "My people have been guilty of two great evils, they have *forsaken* ME, the Fountain of living water, and have hewn *out for themselves broken cisterns*, that can hold no water." And again, "If I am a Father, where is the obedience due to me?" Hear his interrogatory—"If I am a King, where is the honour due to my supremacy?" Is it shown by the substituting of counterfeit and fictitious currency for that standard value which He demands as the tribute due to His name? "On our most sacred day," says the Rabbi, "we implore him, who is our Father and our King, for pardon."

Isaiah assures us that the most solemn days are only aggravations of offence, the very prayers of the double-minded being odious in the sight of Him who demands the whole heart. The Rabbi finds "not the slightest difficulty in arriving at the true meaning of the entire Psalm." It only requires David to be substituted for David's Lord. "The Lord has said unto me (*i.e.*, David), Thou art my son, this day have I begotten thee."!! The ostrich, although notorious for want of wisdom, is said to have the faculty of digesting *iron*—a faculty with which the disciples of the Rabbi would require to be endowed.

The Rabbi having entirely to his own satisfaction assumed that collective Israel is not only the daughter, but the son of *God*, adds, "You will easily understand why, by the employment of the same *metaphor*, the king of Israel, *as representative of the people*, is pre-eminently termed 'the *son of the Lord.*' " By his own showing, the title "son of God" applies only *metaphorically* to the people, and to David only as the people's *representative!!* But it is not so applied to Him whose right it is as בַּר, the *Creator*, essentially one with his Father, the WORD embodied. To the next passage, "Kiss the son, lest he be angry," the Rabbi rather demurs as being of Chaldean origin. Has he then forgotten that the mother tongue of Abraham, being *Chaldean*, he carried it with him as such. If it fell into disuetude ages after, the relative terms (of which it is the root) still remain as בְּרָא, to create, and דָּבָר, to speak—to assert its origin and dignity. "Many Jewish commentators," says the Rabbi, "render this: 'Arm yourselves with purity.'" One we could name renders it, " Kiss a pure one," anything being preferred to the legitimate sense of this very emphatic word. The Rabbi admits that it is found in Proverbs as בַּר, and if so, there is no reason why it should not also be found in the Psalms. He finds that the call to kiss the son applies with perfect propriety to *David* as an act of homage; *i.e.*, "to acknowledge the sovereignty of David, lest the Lord should destroy them in anger."!! How puerile. "The event predicted," says the oracular Rabbi, "came to pass. The Philistines were utterly discomfited, and his (David's) throne firmly established." But does the Rabbi really believe that David's supremacy and inheritance included the uttermost ends of the earth? or that the Philistines served to represent the confederacy of all kings? Those then existing never troubled themselves about, probably never heard of, the law which the prospective rulers shall attempt to abolish. The fact is, that the whole prediction is yet future, as time (the discoverer of events) will show, when "the set time" to favour Zion shall have come.

The Rabbi next turns to the 22nd Psalm, beginning with "*My God, my God, why hast thou forsaken me,*" the only words (from this Psalm) uttered by the Holy One of Israel—the Rabbi having taken leave to add others, in his own mistaken idea that he desired deliverance from the death to which he voluntarily resigned himself as sin-bearer. The deliverance prayed for was by David, who wrote the Psalm (no doubt in some appalling juncture of his own life), centuries before the event which formed the perspective of this dismal picture. The words quoted by the Rabbi are therefore those of the suppliant: "Be not thou far from me, Jehovah, my strength; haste thee to help me, deliver my soul from the sword, my darling from the power of the dog." So far from the willing sin-bearer seeking deliverance from that part of his mission, we find him anticipating the triumphant results of it in these words: "When I shall have been lifted up, I will draw all men to me." Again, "I have a fiery baptism to pass through, and I am straitened until it shall have been accomplished." Here he alludes to that power of dispensing the gifts he should (as conqueror of death) receive at his ascension. His words were those of rebuke to the disciple, who felt grieved and shocked at his intimation of the death awaiting him. "Get thee behind me, adversary, for thou apprehendest not the things of Elohim, but those only of men."

He plainly declared that were such his wish, his Father would send legions of angels to deliver him; but such was not his wish: "Father, forgive them," having been his last words. David says: "Thou wilt not leave my soul in hell, neither wilt thou permit Thy holy one to see corruption." The prophetic spirit of the seer describes (as only that spirit who sees the future as present could), what literally was done by the Roman soldiers: *"They part my garments among them, and cast lots for my vesture."* Rabbi David Kimchi may be very redoubtable as a champion of Rabbinical orthodoxy, and thus to the mind of the Rabbi worthy of all acceptation, but we outsiders consider the Divine oracles all-sufficient as self-interpreters—nay, their very words we hold to be absolutely assertive of the exact truth which they embody.

The disputes occasioned by the terms כְּאֲרִי and כָּאֲרִי "as a lion," may, with great propriety, be left in favour of כָּאֲרִי. The proper term for "*pierce*" or "*stab*" being דָּקַר, and that we find used in allusion to the *same momentous event*. (Zech. xii. 10.) The words, "as a lion they gaped upon me open-mouthed," having been so rendered in the 13th verse, they may with strict propriety have the same rendering in the 17th verse. The homogenity of the hideous scene seems to require this. The guiltless sufferer is described as having been surrounded by his implacable foes, represented by powerful pushing horned animals, their employés as dogs. "Many strong bulls of Bashan have enclosed me—the assembly of the reprobate as a lion have transfixed my hands and feet"—the lion is wont to break the bones of his living prey; but "not a bone of him," who was to rise the third day, could be broken. The Rabbi refers the whole to David, for as already remarked, his landscapes are all foreground, with *no perspective.* Let him speak for himself: "*David represents himself as a carcase attacked by a lion, by bulls, and by dogs,* who are tearing the flesh from his bones, their teeth being fixed in his hands and feet. *The lion is Saul*; the bulls and dogs are his cruel soldiers." . . . He adds, "With *this* explanation, the reading of the 17th verse becomes very simple." The discourse thus perorates: "The *dry bones of dogmatic theology, which Christian expositors would fain discover,* are not enshrined in the Psalms." Nay, more, the "carcase" discovered by the Rabbi is not enshrined there. To those who prefer standard value to any *foreign substitute,* that of "Eternal" (a nonentity) for the glorious NAME, indicating at once BEING and concrete relation, is peculiarly odious; and gratitude for the light and life which first visited "Galilee of the Gentiles" may well constrain us to "speak good of His Name," commended as JEHOVAH's SALVATION, thus fulfilling the prophecy—"*My Name shall be great among the Gentiles.*"

SERMON VI.

Thus begins the Sixth Lecture:—" The Eternal said to my Lord, Sit thou at my right hand, until I make thine enemies thy footstool." The original passage precedes the translated; but even in transcribing the original term, the Rabbinical "dead fly" finds its way into the holy composition, as substituted for the original יְהֹוָה. Such is the enslavement of Rabbinical authority—that baleful covering which has yet to be rent, that Israel may walk in the light of "the law and the testimony." The rendering of Dr. Sach's translation, which the Rabbi prefers, runs thus: "Thy people shall be willing in the day of thy power in holy beauty—out of the bosom of the morning dawn floweth unto thee the dew of thy youth. The Lord hath sworn and will not repent; thou art a priest for ever after the order of Melchizedec. The Lord at thy right hand shall strike through kings on the day of his wrath—he shall judge among the Heathen—he shall fill the places with their dead bodies—he shall crush the heads in the land of Rabbah—he shall drink of the brook in the way, therefore shall he lift up the head." "It is asserted by the Christians," says the Rabbi, "that it contains three distinct predictions concerning the Nazarene." The first verse is *not*, as the Rabbi states, so translated as to *repeat* the term Lord. The capital letters, LORD, being intended for Jehovah; in ordinary letters אֲדֹנָי, personal "Lord." This distinction the Rabbi ignores. The Rabbinical duplicate is a ghost which he cannot lay. The real text is, "Jehovah said to my Adouni, sit thou at My right hand." "Hence it is inferred," says the Rabbi, "that David is predicting the appearance of the Nazarene, already acknowledged as his divinity, and called him 'Lord.' 'He is to sit at the right hand of God.' This expression is alleged to signify that he shall have dominion in heaven and on earth."

Now here again the Rabbi *vitiates* the text, which is not that he *then* sits at the right hand of God, but that "Jehovah at *his right*" hand shall act as described. Heaven is the throne of Jehovah; *renovated* JERUSALEM, *i.e.*, Mount Zion, shall be the throne of His anointed.

The peculiarity of this Psalm, as its title, נְאֻם יְהוָה, indicates, is that it is a direct utterance of JEHOVAH concerning *Adouni* at his right hand; hence David's testimony, " JEHOVAH said to my *Adouni*, Sit thou at My right hand, until I make thine enemies thy footstool."

If in the original text itself, as transcribed by the defender of orthodoxy, a corrupt substitute has intruded in one form—that of *Rabbinical authority*—we need not be surprised to find, in his rendering, a no less fraudulent substitute in another form, that of the *Rationalistic nonentity*, "*Eternal*." Now, as the passage correctly rendered is "JEHOVAH said to my *Adouni*," we can only attribute the assertion of the Rabbi, that "the first verse, said to declare the divinity of the Nazarene, rests on a *mistranslation*," to misconception. That it is untrue is certain, and that the Rabbi may be unconscious that it is so is easily accounted for by his life-long use of the *Rabbinical equivalent*, so long accredited as such, with no authority whatever from recorded Truth. To make the case perfectly clear to every honest mind, it may be needful to show how this counterfeit of the Rabbinical mint became substituted for that standard value which it has so long and deplorably superseded; and in doing so a practical illustration will be afforded of the proverbial fact, that the *first false* step leads to others of the *same* kind.

Here the *first false* step was in the Rabbinical *interdict*, which forbad the *utterance* of that life-giving Name upon which Israel was at all times invited, nay, urged to call. This purblind act, or pious fraud, necessitated the *second false* step, that of *substituting* for the NAME, *which admits of no substitute*, an equivalent—*Adouni* being the term selected: but as that *invariably* denotes *personality*, it underwent a kind of apotheosis (which was supposed to effect a metamorphosis into *impersonal*), and that was by adding the Masoretic vowel sound (ָ) as it stands in Jehovah יְהוָה. This, of course, necessitated a *third false* step, in order to avoid confusion with the *duplicate* term thus fabricated, and that was *wherever* (from Genesis to Malachi) the combined Adouni-Jehovah was found, to substitute the combination Adouni-Elohim, in our version "Lord God." Hence the emphatic and suggestive combination which, as Adouni-Jehovah, tells of BEING and *personality*, is entirely lost sight of. Now, in quoting the passage, the Rabbi, finding himself in a dilemma between *Eternal* (the Rationalistic substitute) and ADONOI (the Rabbinical)—both intended to represent the *interdicted* NAME—the mode of escape to which he betakes himself is, his unwarranted assertion that the mistranslation belongs to those who simply give both words *as they stand recorded*.

Here is the rendering and *aufklärung* of the Rabbi: "The words of the text are not, the *Eternal* speaks to Adonoi"—Adonoi being the word that is often used in the Bible to express Deity—"but to Adouni." Again it may be repeated, Adonoi is not to be found, from Genesis to Malachi, as a *substitute* or equivalent, however often the *personal* term Adouni is *associated* with the great NAME expressive of Divine BEING. It is a remarkable fact that comparatively modern unbelief, in this historical event, should be *satisfied* by the actual national observance which dates from it as such. For while other national events are observed as anniversary celebrations, this national memorial every household (wherever found) strictly and almost daily observes, in refusing to eat of "*the sinew that shrank.*" It will not do to explain away the *fact* thus nationally attested. Rationalists, indeed, take leave to attribute all personal manifestation to a "*heated imagination*," or an "*excited state of brain.*" But neither would account for the life-long physical lameness of Jacob from the "touch of a hand," which left, not only to himself but to his descendants, that lasting memorial. When, therefore, the Rabbi eats as "kosher" the meat from which this peculiar sinew is extracted, let him beware of impiously ignoring as "*fact*," the memorable event which it serves to authenticate.

"Thou art a priest for ever after the order of Melchizedec," is to the mind of the Rabbi only a mataphor, and therefore applicable to a civil ruler.

David being the subject of this psalm, and the scene of his exploits Rabbah, the Rabbi further attributes to him the title of priest. "The expression," he says, "would be applicable to one who needs Divine aid, but is totally inappropriate when used in reference to one who is worshipped as a divinity. "Thou shalt be a priest for ever."—"The word," he adds, "is taken *literally*, and the verse is adduced to prove that this Messiah was to take the place of Aaron's priesthood. . . . Hence one and the same person is the victim that is offered, the high priest who offers it, and the deity to whom it is offered." Assuredly one and the same Being is the priest who offers and to whom the offering of his humanity is acceptable. Can the Rabbi accept the fact that one and the same Being, *i.e.*, the *Divine* WORD, appeared in the burning bush, was the Rock that yielded the people of old streams in the desert, and the Manna which fed them forty years long. "Man did eat angels' food,"—those "who excel in strength through the power of His Word;" that which is our true inner life, and also, in another form, that which sustains it in health and vigour for active service as witnesses to Truth. Nay, more, the Word is the weapon which enables every loyal witness to Truth successfully to vanquish the negative powers of darkness and error.

The Rabbi confounds the Priesthood of the Son of Elohim with that of Aaron; but there cannot be a greater misconception. Of the former it is testified that He shall be a Sovereign and Priest upon His throne, and that *for ever*, and for this reason: that up to the uttermost point of time, through the ages to come, His intercession will be wanted, His priesthood being as much a reality as Himself. The priesthood of Aaron, which has been suspended during this interregnum and its desolations and deviations, shall, we are plainly told, be restored. For, as the sacrifices of guiltless substitutes pointed prospectively of old to the Lamb of Elohim, who should cover, מְכַפֵּר, the sins of the world, so shall they, under the government of the Messiah, point retrospectively to that which signalised the fulness of time; thus realizing the declaration: "The land shall not always remain alienated, because the land is MINE. The Rabbi finds an argument in favour of his own theory of David's priesthood. He says: "The concluding verses speak of battles that will be fought by the personage to whom the psalm is addressed, and of kings whom he will crush. No record exists of battles which the Nazarene fought." As a witness to Truth he was continually in conflict with error in doctrine and hypocrisy in practice. He was at war with all that had overlaid and corrupted the light of the Law and the Testimony. He was like refiner's fire, separating the base from the precious of Divine quality and standard value. Other battles are with confused noise, and garments drenched in blood; His was with burning and heat of fire. Isaiah explains: "For to us a child is born, to us a son is given, and he shall be called miracle פֶּלֶא counsellor, the mighty EL, the perpetual Father, and Prince of Peace."

The Rabbi proceeds to show that it must be David, and that it was composed on the eve of a war, for indignity offered by the Ammonites to David's messengers.

How much more terrible the indignation kindled "for indignity" to the WORD *embodied*, "the Holy One of Israel."

"With these facts before us," says the Rabbi, "all difficulties vanish. As the king goes forth to battle, the spirit of God rests upon one of the minstrels of the royal court, and he proclaims: 'The Eternal saith to my lord, Sit thou at my right hand, until I make thine enemies thy footstool.' The poet pictures the king going forth to battle, surrounded by his youthful warriors, as bright and as numerous as the dew-drops on a summer morn, and willing to shed their blood in his service. 'Thy people shall be willing in the day of thy power, in holy beauty.'" The idea that holy beauty and war and bloodshed are compatible, is a monstrous perversion. "The Psalmist solemnly proclaims how firmly David's sovereignty shall be established:—'Thou art a priest for ever' . . . *i.e.*, a ruler for ever." One would naturally suppose that the Rabbi is here speaking ironically of David in these strangely inappropriate statements. Not so; as the dupe of that potent delusion which *perverted* Truth supplies, he firmly believes his own fallacy.

Has the Rabbi to be reminded that David was not permitted the honour of building the sanctuary. "Thou shalt not build an House unto My Name, for thou hast shed blood in My sight." The Rabbi finds no cause why this should be any hindrance to the far greater honour assigned to David's Adouni, who came as his Root-branch, "not to destroy men's lives, but to save them." Hence the Father's declaration: "Thy throne, Elohim, is for ever, a sceptre of righteousness is the sceptre of thy kingdom. Thou hast loved righteousness and hated iniquity, therefore Elohim, thy Elohim, hath anointed thee with the oil of gladness above thy associates." The Rabbi sees in David the worthy head of a people whose mission it was to become a kingdom of priests. He may rest assured that under the Messiah's rule this prediction will be realized, for then regenerate Israel, as witness-bearers to Truth, shall illustrate as well as proclaim the pure ancestral faith, based as that is on Truth—the Rock of Ages. Meanwhile, let him attend to the question of the prophet: "By whom shall Jacob arise, for he is little, grovelling."

"He shall drink of the brook in the way, therefore shall he lift up the head,"—another expression for the proverb, "Before honour is humility." The Rabbi cannot see it in that light. Priest is with him a metaphor, not a reality, hence it applies better to a warrior than to the Prince of Peace. He says: "It is very absurd applied to the son of the Most High, but quite appropriate in its application to David, whose warriors literally required to drink when on their way to battle." The allusion of the Rabbi to "how much of the brilliant success that attended our recent campaign in Abyssinia was due to the admirable manner in which our troops were supplied with water," is as far-fetched as it is silly. Thus he perorates : "*The prophecy was fulfilled.* David gathered all the people together, and fought against Rabbah and took it. (!!) *My exposition of the psalm is ended.* And now I ask you to judge whether the explanation I have given does not at once sweep away the dogmatic cobwebs with which this psalm has been covered in the process of ages."

The comment of a reverend gentleman seems to astonish the Rabbi. He says: "It is unintelligible to me how the Rev. ——— can say that 'there is no one event in the life of David to which, with the smallest amount of probability, we can assign this psalm.'"

SERMONS VII. AND VIII.

THE Rabbi proposes, as the subject of his Seventh *Aufklärung*, to explain a passage in the book of Daniel; but before his exposition, he calls the attention of his disciples to "a curious instance of the extreme lengths to which Christian theologians go in founding their dogmas on the Bible." It appears that a certain unwise clergyman perplexed a certain uninformed individual in West Canada with the text, "*a threefold cord is not easily broken,*" which, he asserted, contained an unanswerable confirmation of the doctrine of the "*Trinity;*" thus in effect putting a *stumbling-block* in the way of the "*blind.*" (Leviticus xix. 14.) The Rabbi adds: "The poor man, astounded and bewildered, implored that the true significance of this verse might be explained to him." Had this groping soul come under the light of "the Law and the Testimony," instead of expecting help from a distance, he might have been able to say with the Psalmist, "I am wiser than my teachers, because Thy testimony is my meditation." The Rabbi comments on the words, "two are better than one," perfectly unconscious of the value of *quality*, and in the same unconsciousness he adds: "A union of three is yet more advantageous. (!!) I will mention," he continues, "two other passages, one from the prophet Isaiah,"—literally in the Hebrew idiom, it runs: "Adouni Jehovah hath sent me and His spirit." Our version, perfectly preserving the meaning of the passage, renders: "The LORD God, and His Spirit hath sent me," thus recognising the Holy Spirit as a Divine Being, a truth which the Rabbi seeks to neutralise. By recurring to the prophet's initiation and mission, the case is made very plain. When the Adouni said, "Whom shall *we* send, and who will go for *us*," the prophet's response was, "Send me." Hence his declaration to the people: "Adouni Jehovah and HIS SPIRIT hath sent me." Had the SPIRIT not been thus included, the terms "we" and "us" would not have been used. Surely the Rabbi knows or should know that חָכְמָה and Schekinah are identical with the HOLY SPIRIT of whose *sevenfold* energy the seven burning lamps, on the seven branched golden shaft of old, was the symbol and representative.

The next text quoted is, "*I neither learned wisdom or to know the Holy One. Who hath ascended to heaven, or descended? who hath held the wind in his palms? who hath restrained the water in a swathe? who hath founded the extremes of the earth? What is His name? and what is His Son's name?*" To this very telling and many-sided passage this is his comment: "No human being has assisted at the formation of the several elements. (!!) God's omnipotence is unapproachable." The words, 'What is his son's name' are especially introduced," says this sapient authority, "to contrast the human with the Divine Being." Now as the term *son* naturally implies and suggests a relative affinity, that of "waif" would better serve to express the "contrast" to which the Rabbi alludes. He goes on to say that attempts have been made, from a few even garbled passages, to prop up the doctrine of the Trinity, but that "there towers above them all one firm rock, against which the billows of cavil and controversy dash in vain,—the grand verse, 'Hear, O Israel, the *Lord* our *God* is one Eternal Being.'" In this metamorphosed form we can only see a treacherously dangerous *sandbank*, on which אֵין כָּבוֹד is inscribed in foreign phrase. Speed the good time when the Rock of Israel will re-appear in the heart-thrilling sense of its faithfully rendered appeal, HEAR, ISRAEL, JEHOVAH OUR ELOHIM IS ONE JEHOVAH!

While the Rabbi loathingly strains at a "gnat," *i.e.*, the faulty term "Trinity," he swallows with perfect ease a "camel," an orthodox *substitute* for the text transmitted for all time by Moses and the prophets. Hence the peculiar adaptation of his peroration (intended for his Christian neighbours), "add not unto His words, lest He reprove thee, and thou be found a falsifier."

The Rabbi proceeds to deal with the predictions of Daniel the prophet. The "obscurities" he meets with, arise from the fact that, having a theory of his own to eke out as he best can from such unbending integrity of testimony and accuracy of dates, he accepts neither the testimony nor the dates of the prophet. "This obscurity," says the Rabbi, "is due to the fact that the predictions are not direct prophecies like those of Isaiah, but visions." Does he then fancy that to predict and to prophesy are not identical ideas involved in the gift of inspiration? And does he dream that Isaiah's prophecy was not given in vision? His own introductory words sufficiently confirm this fact: "The visions that Isaiah, the son of Amos, saw concerning Judah and Jerusalem." To the misconception thus demonstrated is due the following pendant: "His book is therefore classed among the holy writings, and *not among the prophets.*" Happily, with the written WORD as our STANDARD, we are not left to opinion or conjecture on subjects of vital importance. Having found no warrant to exclude Daniel or his book from the glorious company of the prophets, those worthy protestants who superintended the arrangement of Holy Writ in our version have happily thus been able to recognise in Daniel a distinguished claim to the place he there holds, as one who not alone predicted future events (requiring only time for their realization), but the special date at which their fulfilment should become due as historical facts.

The passage, as rendered by the Rabbi, gives us a note of warning, that of *substituting indefinite* for definite. The theory of the Rabbi requires more than one Anointed (that term answering his purpose better than Messiah), which is limited to the Holy One of Israel; but this is not all,—his theory requires, moreover, that *the people* are to be considered "*the Son of man*," thus coming in the clouds of heaven, *i.e.*, in the glory of the Father (the Schekinah) and his own glory, that " cloud of witnesses to Truth " which He claims as His special crown of rejoicing. The pantheistic monomania of the Rabbi thus finds expression: " It is clear from these words, *i.e.*, ' The kingdom, dominion, and supremacy of the kingdom under the whole heaven, shall be given to the people of the saints of the Most High,' *that by the term Son of Man a people, and not an individual, is to be understood,*" and this clue (which certainly defies logical requirement) the Rabbi finds in " the *four beasts* which were not *creatures but kingdoms.*" The Rabbi evidently expects that under this regime a republican or democratic form of government (that which the supreme people may decree), shall then have superseded the Theocratic administration!! But happily the saints of the Most High, who stand in the relation of His beloved, the sharer of His sufferings as witness to truth, and of His regal glory as conqueror of death, will act according to His will who is her Head and Governor. Had the theorist considered the import of the original terms בְּכַר אֲנָשׁ he could not have fallen into a blunder alike damaging to his credit as a teacher and a Hebrew scholar. Surely, had he done so, he would have felt it impossible thus to trifle with a word implying the Creator, the Divine Word בַּר being, as he knows, the root of

דָּבַר (to speak) and בָּרָא (to create), as already stated. To attribute this essentially and exclusively Divine title to the saints of the Most High would be at once impious and absurd; how much more so, when assumed for the yet *unregenerate people*. "To whom will ye liken me, saith Jehovah?" Surely not to his guilty creatures. The coming in the clouds of heaven is rather an inconvenient situation for the *pantheist Son of Man;* so to obviate that difficulty the Rabbi reduces the Schekinah to a phrase, *i.e.*, "the decree of heaven."

The Rabbi having thus exhausted, to his own satisfaction, the 13th and 14th verses of the 7th chapter, proceeds to the 24th and 25th of the 9th chapter. Amongst other commentators, he mentions three *noted rationalists*, Langerke, Hitzic, and Ewald, whom he has found helpful.

The inspired prophet thus announces the information vouchsafed to him, as the effect of fervent prayer to Adouni-Jehovah, the hearer and answerer of prayer: "Seventy-sevens (of years) are determined upon thy people, and upon thy holy city, to finish transgression, to make reconciliation כָּפַר (covering) for iniquity עָוֹן, to inaugurate everlasting righteousness, to seal up the vision and prophecy, and to anoint the holy of holies, (in our translation 'most holy.')" As the prediction is inseparably connected with the Land and its *seren* (rest and release) *years*—thus integrally related—each portion must, of necessity, have its fulfilment in the Land. Hence the prophet's suggestive mode of notifying each salient event, due to each period. The first portion of the period specified, *i.e.*, 49 years, or "*seven sevens*," is that assigned for the *rebuilding of the Sanctuary*, beginning to reckon from the edict of Cyrus. The second period, of 434 years, gives time for the increase of that corruption, in doctrine and practice, which would culminate in the prediction due, as matter of history, to that generation of wrath, whom its visitation found totally unprepared.

The prophet's words are: "After threescore and two sevens shall the Messiah be cut off, but not for himself; and the prince of the people that shall come shall destroy the city and the sanctuary, and until the end desolations are determined. History tells us this predestined destruction of the sanctuary by "the people" of the invading prince was by *fire* (a soldier having thus unconsciously fulfilled the sentence that had gone forth). The dispersion of the misled people soon followed. And thus did the present interregnum become an interval of occupancy, and probation to this Western Empire. The *destruction*—by the Roman power, before it had assumed its last phase, that of ecclesiastical mistress of the world, under a foreign head—should not be confounded with the desecration foretold by Daniel. In recurring to the "seventy sevens," or 490 years, we shall find that the two periods of 49 and 434 years, together 483 years, leave "*one seven*" *years* for *future* fulfilment, however long the interregnum (caused by the desolation of the Land now enjoying its rests or Sabbaths). This "seven," being an *integral* portion of the whole, must necessarily (as the winding-up scene of that drama of which Jerusalem shall be the theatre), become due at the close of this interlude of the Gentile nations.

Daniel informs us that in the midst of the "seven" (reserved years), the *then* ruler shall perfidiously *ignore* the treaty into which he had entered with the newly restored people, and at the end of 3½ years not only abolish the statutes and ordinances of the land, but— to prove his own supreme authority—set up in the sanctuary his tutelary deity, "the god of forces."

Thus shall that brief period witness those terrific events described as "the days of vengeance," "the time of Jacob's trouble."

The words of our supreme Teacher point to this very epoch. The words He uses are designed to show His immediate hearers that His warning was for those who should "*read*" not hear (as they did) this forewarning. "When, therefore, ye shall see the abomination of desolation predicted by Daniel the prophet—(*let him that readeth, understand*)—then let them that be in Judea flee to the mountains, and let him on the housetop not come down to take anything out of the house, neither let him that is in the field return to take his clothes." Immediately after the tribulation of *those days* shall the sun be darkened, and the moon shall withhold her light . . . . and there shall appear the אוֹת of the Son of Man in heaven, and then shall all the tribes of the land mourn, for they shall see "the Son of Man" coming in the clouds of heaven, with power and great glory, and He shall send His messengers with the great sound of the הָרְוּעָה, and they shall gather His elect from the four winds, from one extreme under heaven to the other. Therefore be ye ready, for in such an hour as ye think not, the Son of Man cometh ; who then is a faithful and wise servant, whom his Lord hath made ruler over the household, to give them their portion of food in due season."

The immediate judgment caused by the impious act of the wilful king is the earthquake described by Zechariah, and thus alluded to: " Ye shall flee as ye fled from the earthquake in the days of Uzziah, . . . and Jehovah, my Elohim, shall come, and all the saints with him."

The theory of the Rabbi, alike regardless of anomalies and of anachronisms, requires that during the 49 years (assigned by the prophet for one event, *i.e.*, the rebuilding of the sanctuary), one anointed should be a temporal prince, and that another should be cut off and *be no more* (for so he renders וְאֵין לוֹ), and as he takes leave to elect Cyrus for the former, so Onias, the high priest (who was put to death through the treachery of Menelaus during the tyranny of Antiochus Epiphenes), serves equally well for the latter. The Rabbi lays much stress on the division of this first portion from the 434 which follow. " It is," he says, " divided by a sign or point which has all the force of a colon." Now, however important this point may be to the theory of the Rabbi, it has nothing whatever to do with the original record, *that* having been penned long before this *artificial sign* was invented. The Rabbi says : " This vision was to announce to them that at the expiration of 490 years after the destruction of the temple, their sufferings *would be at an end!* their iniquity pardoned! the piety and righteousness of old re-established ! and the holy of holies again anointed !" He adds : " The prophet here foretells events which *were fulfilled* . . . by Judas Maccabæus, and the re-establishment shortly afterwards of the *independence* of Israel, when kings of their own race and faith sat upon the throne of David, and a new era commenced . . . the era of the freedom of Israel." ! !

Now did this fulfil the prediction ? did it *finish* the transgression ? So far from that, it only reached its full measure some centuries after. "To make an end of sin, and make reconciliation כַּפֵּר (cover) iniquity." Before the peace-offering was made, was everlasting righteousness brought in ? Did any of all these events take place *then*, before iniquity and corruption had attained its last stages of development?

To talk of *that* as the era of Israel's freedom is absurd. Under the Roman power, as tributaries, they had neither king or independent priesthood, the Sanhedrin having, under that power, attained its acme of corrupt and sinister subservience.*

He seems to have a dim inkling that his theory will not stand investigation. He says: "The above I conceive to be a correct explanation of this obscure prophecy. I cannot assert that the dates of these events . . . . coincide *exactly* with the years here indicated. . . . But the one important point which I trust I have demonstrated to you is, that the Christian interpretation of the passage *is quite incorrect*. He adds: " While for us it would be perfectly permissible to say that this prophecy is *an enigma which defies solution*, those who consider it a corner stone **of their faith** should be able clearly and unhesitatingly to unravel the meaning of every phrase comprised in it."

Those most likely to perceive clearly what is hid from eyes that will "not perceive" are such as simply believe, without cavil or question, what Daniel testifies. To such it is as plain as that two and two make four, that two predicted events had centuries ago become historical facts. One, the rebuilding of the Temple, the other, Messiah cut off, the last "seven" being reserved for the *desecration* of a Temple *not yet built* but already subscribed for, **by those whom** political events (now rapidly in the course of evil development) **may drive to that** terrible scene described in the 2nd Psalm.

It is to this political gathering that the following declaration refers:—"Thus saith Adouni Jehovah, because ye are all become dross, therefore I will gather you into the midst of Jerusalem, as they **gather silver, and brass, and iron,** and lead, and tin, in the midst of **the furnace, to blow the fire** upon them, to melt them; yea, I will **gather you, to blow upon you in the fire** of My wrath, and ye shall be *melted therein*. **And it shall come to** pass that they that are left in Zion, and that **remain in Jerusalem shall** be called holy, every one written among the **living in Jerusalem**." (Ezekiel xx. 19.) "On that day the Branch of Jehovah shall be in beauty and glory. . . for them that are preserved of Israel." (Isaiah iv. 3, 4.)

It appears that so-called Christian rulers will act in direct antagonism to the Divine will, in their attempts to get rid of the statutes and ordinances of the land. Hence the declaration, "I will make

---

* Caiaphas and others were in fact put into office by the Roman governor of that day.

Jerusalem a cup of delirium to all peoples, when they shall be in the siege against Judah and Jerusalem, all that burden themselves with it shall be cut into fragments. Then shall the governors of Judah say in their heart, there is strength for me and the inhabitants of Jerusalem in Jehovah of hosts, their Elohim. In that day will I make the governors of Judah like a **hearth** of fire among wood, and **like a torch** of fire in straw, ... and Jerusalem shall again be inhabited in her own place." Then follows the effusion of the Holy Spirit in the grace of prayer and supplication. And then, "Comfort ye, comfort ye my people, speak comfortingly to Jerusalem, for her warfare is then accomplished, her iniquity pardoned. Behold Adouni Jehovah shall come against the mighty, His reward is *then* with Him, He shall feed His flock like a shepherd, and He shall gather the lambs." (Isaiah xl.)

The concluding words of this sermon show the whereabouts of leader and led: "Yes, brethren, if we would *learn how to gain eternal bliss for ourselves*, we must turn to the Torah, the Law of God." In turning to that condemnatory light, what confronts the transgressor? Inexorable justice. For while the law is light and life to the *regenerate* who *know* and *do* the Father's *will* with a single eye to His glory (their righteousness, like that of Abraham, being of faith), it is *death* to the wilful rejector of Jehovah's salvation. Hence the declaration: "Israel, thou hast destroyed thyself, but in ME is thy strength found; their righteousness is of ME, saith יְהוָֹה."

SERMON IX.

The Ninth Sermon begins thus: "In expounding to you the principal of the so-called Christological passages in the Bible, I have, I trust, succeeded in proving to you that not only do they not apply to him whom Christians believe to be their redeemer, but they do not apply to a Messiah." A rather startling assertion, after the Rabbi had ferreted out two *substitutes*, to one of whom he took leave to apply the prediction of Daniel: "*Messiah shall be cut off, but not for himself.*" "Holy Writ," says the Rabbi, "speaks of a Redeemer who will come, but who has not yet appeared on earth. The Bible," he adds, "does contain predictions, couched in plain and distinct language, concerning the advent of the true Redeemer, at whose appearance Israel shall be gathered together, and again be united to form a happy and prosperous nation." The Rabbi seems to overlook the fact that the prophets who foretold this *eventual* gathering, also foretold the scattering which should *precede* it. "Awake, sword, against My shepherd, the man My associate; smite the shepherd, that the sheep may be scattered." Again, the Rabbi may read in very plain and distinct language, "*HE who scattered Israel shall gather them,*" as a shepherd gathers his flock. The Rabbi may **shut** his eyes to this aspect of one and *the same* Redeemer's ministry and mission; he may *close* his ears against this *manifest historical fact*, but if **he refuses to hear** the voice of Divine Wisdom, "charm she ever so wisely," he does so at his own peril. If at one time, as "the *Lamb* of Elohim, the Redeemer came to *take away the curse due to sin by* making *humankind his purchased property;* at *another time*, as the "Lion of Judah," he will come to "reckon" with the leaseholders for the light, either accepted as a guide in wisdom's way, or ignored, resisted, or perverted,—invoked as *condemnation;* that same coming as Judge to the nations being for the redemption of his then willing people. Hence the declaration: "*The day of vengeance is in Mine heart*, and the year of My redeemed is come." Every true believer in Scripture testimony accetps, without cavil, "all that the prophets have spoken."

The Rabbi admits that certain ancient commentators do explain some prophetic statements *differently* in the Targum, &c., but his *ipse dixit* being all the panoply required by his congregants, he avoids any dangerous enquiry to which further notice of these *differences* might lead. The fact is, that the ancient Rabbins had not been inoculated (as many moderns have been) with rationalism. They were more apt to "add" than to "subtract" from the all-sufficient measure of revealed truth. It was reserved for the successive bands of rationalistic German theorists—if Jews, under the special leadership of Maimonides, "the father of every artificer in rationalism and *aufklärung*"—to "explain away," *i.e.*, to reduce to *nil*, whatever did not accord with their mental intuition and arbitrary modes of thinking. What, therefore, is to be expected of the worshippers of a leader who makes prophecy depend partly upon natural conformation and partly on art.*

The Rabbi quotes from Isaiah xi., 1st and 9th verses: "There shall come a ROD out of the *stem* of Jesse, and a *branch* shall grow out of his ROOTS;" proceeding thus: "Let me now show you how impossible it is that the personage here referred to can be the Nazarene. The prophet predicts that the Messiah will be a scion of the house of David,—Christianity declares its Redeemer to be of Divine origin." Having quoted the whole passage, he continues in oracular tone: "Now peruse carefully the whole prophecy, and you will not discover a word which can imply that the Redeemer is of Divine origin." Had an intelligent lad of twelve years old, as בַּר מִצְוָה, availed himself of the ancient privilege of putting questions, he might have asked, "To what, if not to a Divine person, does the prophet allude in these words: 'He shall smite the earth with the rod of His mouth, and with the breath of His lips shall He slay the rebels?'" If somewhat well-informed—a rare thing in the present age—he would have added, "the same prophet applies this very language to the Almighty." The *beau ideal* of the Rabbi is (parentage included) strictly *mundane*, yet he is "not to be a man of ordinary qualifications." ! !

---

* Si fuerit homo cujus cerebre substantia in decenti perfectione et respectu materiæ temperamenti proportionis et locationis . . . si postea studeat.—Moreh Nevuchim, part ii., chap. 45.

The Rabbi will find that there is ample warrant for our belief in the Divine origin of the person alluded to by Isaiah. Jeremiah, inspired by the same Spirit, thus testifies: "I will raise up unto David a *righteous branch*, ('scion,' if the Rabbi prefers it,) . . . and in His day shall Judah be delivered, and Israel shall dwell safely. And this is His NAME by which He shall be called, JEHOVAH our Righteousness." The 10th verse thus encourages our faith in our glorious Redeemer: "In that day shall there be a root of Jesse, which shall stand for an ensign of the people. To Him shall the Gentiles attach themselves, and His Rest shall be glorious." Malachi thus expresses the same fact, due to future history: "His NAME shall be great among the Gentiles." Before the blight of rationalism had fallen upon the European Hebrews, this Hope of Israel was kept alive in the pious breathings of devout souls. One instance may suffice to show this, in an exquisitely simple yet most sublime hymn, which is intoned in every synagogue throughout the world. Confronted in his own synagogue by such a telling memorialist, how can the Rabbi stifle the emotion which its heart-thrilling appeal to the Holy One of Israel calls forth:—

Thou art our Elohim	אַתָּה אֱלֹהֵנוּ
Thou art our Adouni	אַתָּה אֲדֹנֵנוּ
Thou art our King	אַתָּה מַלְכֵּנוּ
Thou art our Messiah	אַתָּה מוֹשִׁיעֵנוּ

This is evidently not the Messiah modern materialists look for. But happily a deep under-current exists, and for the resuscitation of the people, these are now required to act as free men in behalf of truth.

The old commentators (apt as they were to indulge in addenda and crotchets), never attempted to reduce to the level of our negative earthly nature the promised "seed of the woman," born to retrieve the disasters of man's transgression. In Him, they saw the reclaimer of forfeited dominion, and earth's universal ruler. The Jerusalem Targum, Kimchi, Abarbanel, Tanchum, and the whole consensus of Jewish commentators, proclaim, as with one voice, זֶה הַמֶּלֶךְ הַמָּשִׁיחַ this is the King Messiah. Both the Targum and the Talmud speak of His human birth, both speak of His dominion. Micah describes His going forth from ancient times—hence His title, the "Ancient of days," in affinity with the "Son of Man," whose dominion was to be "under the whole heaven." Ben Ezra hesitates between David and Messiah, his root and offspring. But the Targum, David Kimchi, and even R. Isaac, in the "Chizzuk Emunah," explain it positively of Messiah. It cannot apply to an earthly king. The anointing by the Divine Spirit, the righteousness of the king, the universality of his rule, and the eternal praise awaiting and due to him from the eventually regenerate nations—are applicable to the Messiah alone. Kimchi says plainly that it is the Messiah, whose name is mentioned in all generations.

Certain old writers affirm that the Messiah was born before the destruction of the Second Temple. Where He is now they know not, but say that He will assuredly appear at the time appointed. It is added, "May their souls be confounded who compute the time." The Name—the Branch—was universally applied to the Messiah. The Targum on Hosea iii. 5, Jer. xxx. 9, puts Messiah for דָּוִד David. The Talmud (Sanhedrin ix. 13), proves from Ezekiel xxxiv. 23, 24, that David should be the name of the Messiah.

Can the Rabbi tell who, if not the "Messiah cut off," as the disembodied Word, entered the domain of the dead? Who, but man's Redeemer, can use such language as the following: "I will ransom them from the power of Sheol, I will redeem them from death. Death, I will be thy destroyer! Sheol, I will be thy Devastator!"* Of whom but this Hero, armed with righteous warrant to reclaim His purchase, could it have been said, "Thou hast ascended up on high, thou hast led captivity captive; thou hast received gifts בָּאָדָם even for the rebellious, that Elohim might dwell with them." How could the mission and ministry of the embodied Word have been fulfilled, as proclaimer of eventual "liberty to the captives, the opening of the prison to them that are bound," had He not descended into the lower parts of the earth, *i.e.*, Sheol. Again, who, if not the ascended conqueror of death, thus speaks as intercessor: "For Zion's sake I will not be silent, for Jerusalem's sake I will not rest, until her righteousness shall go forth in splendour, and her salvation as a lamp that burneth; and the nations shall see her light, and all kings her glory."

The Rabbi states that the restoration of Israel, which must one day be fulfilled, was not accomplished during the life-time of the

---

* Hosea xiii. 14.

Nazarene. Does he require to be reminded that there is a time to scatter and a time to gather; a time to sow mournfully under a dark horizon, and a time to reap joyfully under sevenfold light. Hence the declaration, "He who went forth to sow in tears shall assuredly return with joy, bringing with him his gathered sheaves." Hence also the declaration, "He who scattered Israel shall gather them, as a shepherd gathers his flock unto their own fold."

The Rabbi has good reason for reprehending the dishonest practice to which some of our commentators have resorted, that of attempting to *accommodate* prophetic testimony to our interlude, and the foreign relation and constitution of this last world-empire, destined to dissolution in its last phase—the wolf in sheep's guise.

His rebuke is less severe than this offence against truth and reason would justify. "To explain prophecies which foretell the *calamity* in accordance with the *literal* meaning, and yet place a *metaphorical* construction upon those which announce their future felicity," is indeed "contrary to all sound interpretation." Nay, it is truth *perverted* into that potent delusion which in effect turns the blessing of its *integrity* into a self-made curse, inasmuch as every attempt to "*wrest*" the testimony or structure of the recorded Word is suicidal.

SERMON X.

The Rabbi begins his Tenth *Aufklärung* with a quotation from the prophet Micah, iv. 1—4. He thus proceeds: "As these glorious predictions pass before my mind's eye, the question suggests itself —have any of them been fulfilled?" Were the Rabbi better acquainted with prophetic testimony as an inviolable whole, he would not expect those bright visions of future peace—the fruit of righteousness—to be realized while yet the last foredoomed world-dominion exists.

The kingdom for which we are taught to pray—predestined to supersede its evil elements, constitution and character—must, as the object of our well-founded faith, as the polar star which guides the mariner—be our continual object of hopeful, joyful trust. It is not for want of the manifestation of Divine light (in the form best suited to the existing exigency) that either Jews or Gentiles have continued to prove what they are, in their direct antagonism to that life-giving light. The fact being plainly this, that men have *preferred* darkness (of their own originating) to the light, because, their nature being perverse, their deeds are evil. Can the Rabbi tell why the voice of Jehovah has continually, on one pretext or another, been ignored. They who have ever done so, could tolerate the Divine Word in the *recorded form*; even superstition and devotional ignorance could worship it as a kind of idol, bedecked, belled, and thus worthy of unthinking homage. But when did the same Word receive heart-homage as the Divine voice in personal form? Thus was Moses instructed to speak to his disobedient and gainsaying people: "Now, therefore, if ye will *obey My voice* and *keep My covenant*, then shall ye be unto Me a *special* treasure, for all the earth is mine." What is the historical fact to which the long continued degradation of the nation testifies? This—that they refused to listen to that voice, either uttered by Jehovah or by messengers who spake in His Name. What is His own testimony? "My covenant they brake, though I was an husband unto them."

Now all this perverse disregard of the Divine Word cannot with justice be urged by the deist or materialist as a proof that there was *no manifestation of the Divine Being*, whose voice proclaimed and whose hand recorded His law. To His people it only serves to prove that until the heart—whence proceed the issues of life—is reclaimed from misleading influences to the *loving obedience of sonship*, man is a self-deceived rebel; hence the nations by whom the Divine light has been practically ignored, resisted, or **perverted**, are self-prepared for the last manifestation of judicial blindness— national madness. To blame the sun for those **offensive qualities** which his beneficent **warmth draws forth from** *corrupt matter* would be worse than foolish, it would betray *enmity* to essential good.

"Turn where we may," continues the Rabbi, "do we not see the reign of violence and lawlessness still prevails, that might still triumphs over right? . . . We see the most powerful and civilized nations vieing with one another in the production of the deadliest* weapons of destruction. How much wealth and skill are wasted day by day in order that the deep-mouthed cannon may with greater accuracy hurl forth death and destruction on its doomed victims! Aye, whoever throws a glance at the history of the world, must acknowledge that the eighteen centuries which have elapsed since the supposed appearance of the Messiah, present a sad and discouraging aspect. Does not the earth still drink the blood of her children? *How, then, can it be asserted that the Messiah has already come?*" Let us hear what the Prince of Peace expects at the hands of Christendom, and of nations who belie alike his name, doctrine and example. "As it was in the days of Noah, so shall it

---

* When the Rabbi, who seems to execrate the production of deadly weapons of destruction by "powerful and civilized nations," in the same breath talks of returning thanksgiving to the Father of *all* for what he fulsomely calls the "*brilliant triumph*" of *our forces* in Abyssinia, the "proud traditions of *British* valour," &c., he seems oblivious of the fact that, for *such* triumphs and traditions, these murderous weapons of brute force power are *indispensable*. And here, too, he totally misunderstands the staple quality of British character, that of a backbone manliness which would respect the honest friend who shows their national faults and inconsistencies, while detesting equivocal eulogy. Let the Rabbi be advised to feel as Abraham did, and as the heirs of promise must ever do, *i.e.*, as "strangers and pilgrims," the expectants of a kingdom of righteousness and peace, wherein our Heavenly Father's will shall be the central spring of all loyal hearts.

be in the day when the Son of man is manifested." Then "the earth was covered with violence." Noah proclaimed retributive judgment, but to no purpose. They only awoke to conscious danger when the flood swept them from earth's desecrated face. When nations long favoured with light from above remain utterly unconscious of the claims, the quality, the transforming effects of revealed truth, they are left to fill up the measure of their provocation, for not only scientific discovery, but every effort of godless intellect, serves but to ripen the world for judgment. Who can assign limits to the aggressive spirit of nationalities, under the delirium of their false stimuli? What nation is safe from its internal elements of destruction? If judgment began with the covenant people, what shall be the end of those who " stand by faith," or trustless " fall." " Some of them," continues the Rabbi, " contend that all these glorious promises are to be fulfilled at a second advent of the Nazarene, when, with his saints, he will reign a thousand years upon earth. This is the doctrine of the so-called Millennium. But not a single clear and unequivocal prophecy can be produced from the Bible which foretells a twofold coming of one and the same person as the Messiah. The whole scheme of the Millennium must be declared a chimera, an *ignus fatuus* to delude the unwary."

It must be the *Latin* disguise of the *seventh Aleph* or thousand which so startles the Rabbi, who surely cannot but know that the seventh weekly sabbath-day is but the *type* and *foreshadow* of that Rest or Sabbatism destined to close the six thousand "tardy and disastrous years" of this evil world. To what, but this future good, does the inspired Psalmist thus allude : " *Now* if ye will hear His voice, *harden not your heart*, as in the provocation, in the day of trial in the wilderness; when your fathers tried Me, proved Me, and saw My works. Forty years long was I grieved with *that* generation, and said, It is a people that do *err in their hearts*, for they have *not known My ways*. Unto whom I sware in my wrath, that they should not enter into My אֶל־מְנוּחָתִי place of rest." Through faith Abraham and the other heirs of promise secured an entrance to that future resting-place, while to want of trust in the Divine word of promise is alike due this terrible sentence and the exclusion thus invoked. The Rabbi will find in Psalm cxviii. 22, " a plain and unequivocal prophecy" of this rest, combined with the Messiah, as Lord of the Sabbath, and moreover with those antecedents which prove two different visitations—the former in "the fulness of time," or fourth Aleph, the latter at the close of the sixth of this world's history. "This is the day JEHOVAH hath עָשָׂה prepared, perfected, we will rejoice and be glad in it." " The stone which the builders rejected, is become head of the corner." " This is the doing of JEHOVAH, and it is marvellous in our sight!" " Blessed is He that cometh in Jehovah's name!" There the period of rejection by the builders is referred to as a *past* event, while the coming, as universal **Ruler, is** described as future. The type and antitype, *i.e.*, **the seventh day** and the seventh millenary, bear the **same analogy: the *preparatory* eve and dark midnight preceding the Rest-day of Jehovah.** "*From evening to evening shall your Sabbath be*," holding good of the antitype as of the type. Hence the necessity of being ready with **newly replenished and** newly lighted lamps, to meet the bridal **array so long** and so ardently expected by loyal hearts. If the Rabbi will not accept the evidence thus adduced as a reply to his demand for plain testimony, substantiated by historical fact, his mental blindness must be judicial; such only could remain proof against its Divine power.

The Rabbi having quoted the prediction of Balaam, proceeds: " It is indeed noteworthy with what avidity Christian theologians **seize** upon this passage, purposely veiled. It is stated that this Star of Jacob would wage war with the adjacent nations, Moab **and** Edom. *There is no record, however, of the Nazarene having been engaged in warfare.*" Does the Rabbi require to be reminded **that there** is moral as well as physical power ? and that the Holy One of Israel, wielding **no weapon** but the WORD, waged continual war against the **powers of evil** and darkness? The Star and Sceptre foreseen by Jacob was to **have *universal* dominion;** his kingdom of righteousness and peace being predestined to *supersede* the political constitution and elements of this evil world and its false glory. " There can be little doubt," continues the Rabbi, " that the prediction was verified in the person of David: there may also, perhaps, **be a** hidden reference to the Messiah, the latest of Jacob's descendants. (! !) Let me now call your attention to the book of Micah, **v. 1.** Christians tell us that this prediction has been clearly fulfilled in the person of their Messiah, born at Bethlehem." A circumstance which he takes leave to call accidental, and therefore of no essential or historical **value.** That an event so stupendous in its design, and so momentous to human kind in its issue, would be notified in a remarkable manner, seems indisputable, and so it was: for in the most emphatic manner the decree of Augustus Cæsar compelled the lingering remnants of the house of David to present themselves at Bethlehem for enrolment as tributaries of the Roman power. It was imperative that Miriam, of David's lineage, should with her own hand substantiate the descent of "the child there to be born, the son there to be given;" hence the fulfilment of the promised " woman's seed," the " reclaimer of forfeited dominion," nevertheless, in accordance with prophecy, born tributary and subject to the then ruling power. " A servant of rulers " in this world, but not of it.

Whether we consider the announcement of this event to the shepherds, while by night watching their flocks on the plains of Bethlehem, or the salutation to Miriam nine months before the birth of that world-wide benefactor—all is in perfect harmony. The highest honours from above, the deepest humiliation from beneath. Born in a stable, cradled in a manger. The children of light exulting, the powers of darkness showing their malignity. To the shepherds the greeting of the heavenly host was, "Unto you is born this day in the city of David a Saviour, who is Messiah, the Adouni;" He whose going forth (as messenger of the covenant) had been from עוֹלָם, now, in the person of the woman-born Redeemer, came to confirm the broken covenant, and thus fulfil the will and consummate the purpose of the Most High. To Miriam had been announced, nine months before, this long promised hope, which heralded by angels, accepted by Eastern sages, and notified by the unconcious agency of the Roman Cæsar, had become due as a historical fact, indicating a new epoch, chronicling the fulness of time. Hence the announcement by the same messenger (who, centuries before, had been sent on an errand confirmatory of this hope to the prophet Daniel), to Miriam, the blessed of woman-kind. This salutation of the heavenly messenger was, "Behold thou shalt conceive and bring forth a son, and shalt call his name יְהוֹשֻׁעַ. He shall be great, and shall be called the son of the Most High, and Adouni-JEHOVAH shall give to him the Throne of his father David, and He shall rule over the house of Jacob for ever." And Miriam said, "Behold the handmaid of JEHOVAH, be it unto me according to His word." As the Holy Spirit, from the lips of Miriam, of old had given utterance to a thanksgiving worthy of the deliverance of her people from mortal bondage, so, from the lips of her whom all generations shall call blessed, the Holy Spirit thus gave utterance to a heart-loyalty in which intense devotion, patriotic fervour, and ancestral affection combine. "My soul doth magnify JEHOVAH, my spirit hath rejoiced in ELOHIM my Saviour; for He hath regarded the low estate of His hand-maiden, for from henceforth all generations shall call me blessed. He that is mighty hath done great things for me, and holy is HIS NAME; for His mercy is upon those who fear Him, from generation to generation. He hath showed strength with His arm, He hath scattered the proud in the imagination of their heart; He hath put down the rulers from their throne, and exalted those of lowly estate. The hungry hath He filled with good things, and the rich hath He sent empty away. He hath given help to His servant Israel in remembrance of His grace, as He promised our forefathers, Abraham and his seed for ever." That this magnificent thanksgiving refers only to the regal fulfilment of prophetic testimony, is clear. The Spirit carried her thoughts to the glorious goal. The sorrowful foreground of that bright picture of national prosperity, then hid from her eyes, was thus revealed by one who waited for the consolation of Israel. "Behold," said the aged Simeon, "this child shall be for the fall and rise again of many in Israel, and for a אוֹת, a sign to be maligned; yea, a sword shall pierce thy soul also, that the thoughts of many hearts may be revealed." Thus did the heavenly-minded Hebrew maiden become apprised that the ultimate glory of the champion, predestined to bruise the serpent's head, was to be attained through a self-sacrificing triumph of the Father's will which he embodied.

In winding up his anomalous discourse, the Rabbi, as further evidence that the Prince of Peace has not yet appeared, states that upwards of "half of her majesty the Queen's subjects are heathens," and that "there is no building large enough to hold the idols that are still worshipped." Well it is for the heathen that natural *ignorance* is a pardonable state; happily for them grace finds a plea in their behalf because of that very ignorance of the light they never resisted. Far otherwise with those of whom resisted light is the condemnation.

> "He will not punish, in one mingled crowd,
> Those without light, and thee without a cloud."

Has the Rabbi to learn that the " fetish " of heathen worship are less condemnatory to them, and less odious to Him who judges men according to the light they have (that which shows His mind and will), than the idol-*substitutes* to which those who **have a name to live**—while in reality dead—render practical homage, while the Creator and Redeemer, who claims the whole heart, is insulted with mere lip-service and heartless profession. Ourselves we may deceive—our righteous **Judge** we cannot. Of that which we individually sow we *must* reap. "They who" now "sow the wind shall reap the whirlwind." They who now sow to self and the world, shall reap corruption and remorse.

SERMON XI.

The Eleventh Discourse begins with Zechariah ix. 9. "Granting the historical truthfulness of this record, I assert," says the Rabbi, "that the fact of the Nazarene having entered into Jerusalem, riding upon an ass, is no proof of his being the Messiah promised; knowing well as he did the prophecy, he acted in such a way as to fulfil it." The supreme aim, object and end of the Messiah's mission and ministry having been the *glorification* of TRUTH, he necessarily sought to fulfil all that the prophets had testified of his suffering advent. In his imputation of *sinister* motives and *fraudulent* designs, the Rabbi must therefore be left to draw *entirely* on his own credit and resources.

In the fulfilment of prophetic testimony, unconscious agents, incapable of higher thought than self-interest, have been employed. Such were the Roman soldiers, who "divided among them his garments, casting lots for his vesture;" while the rich councillor of Aramathea—whether inspired by higher motives, or merely by benevolent feeling and detestation of wrong-doing, is left to conjecture—little wist, when he had the rock sepulchre hewn out in his garden, that it should for three days be tenanted by that incorruptible frame, destined anew to become the human sanctuary of JEHOVAH. The fulfilment of prophecy (to the very letter and minutest particular), has, wonderful to say, been effected in the exercise of the most malignant feelings to which persecuting zeal could give birth. Let the Rabbi compare the prediction, which preceded its fulfilment five centuries, and thus learn to form a wiser estimate of prophetic testimony. Then the priests and the Sanhedrin, alike estranged from the pure ancestral faith and doctrine, were corrupt beyond reclaim;—thus their threatened visitation found them ripe for the judgment which their culminating act brought upon leaders and led. The prophecy could not more indisputably have expressed itself; the reputed guardians and custodians of the holy house having paid out of its sacred treasury * the thirty pieces of silver, due as the price of innocent blood, to the betrayer. Nor did they seem to have questioned this impious act of expediency, until the conscience-striken felon, incapable of retaining the accursed thing, or surviving his infamy, returned it to his accomplices (in the Temple), who expended the valuation-sum on the purchase of a field of bad fame, that of the "potter," wherein strangers were to be buried. Hence we read of the "potter's field" alike in the earlier and later record of truth.

The fact of having entered Jerusalam in the manner predicted was perfectly consistent with the humiliation manifested from his manger-cradle in the stable of Bethlehem to his death upon the cross, as a world-wide peace-offering. As the Lamb of Elohim, his voice was not to be heard in the streets; the bruised reed he did not break, the smoking flax he did not quench. Peace was his mission, peace his doctrine and practice. Salvation was his errend; reclaim and the extinction of evil his consummatory triumph. In strong antithesis is his second advent, as Lion of Judah. Then shall He assert His rightful sovereignty over the confederate rulers of the world. Then, also, shall He reckon with the leaseholders, whose term of occupancy and probation shall then close in retributive judgment.

The Rabbi expects, as the result of the Messiah's reign, that "the Eternal will be one." He may rest assured that negation shall then have ceased to offend as a substitute for the life-giving Name. The errand of Elijah will be what it formerly was—corrective.

Then Elijah protested against one kind of illegal *substitute;* again will he protest against all Rabbinical substitutes and devices. What he said then he may well repeat to those whose deviation is from the central Will and Word—the source of Life! We are told explicitly that his final mission will be to *restore* the ancestral faith, so long overlaid by the darkening traditions and misleading comments and burdensome requirements of so-called sages. Elijah knew nothing of the modern nonentity, "Eternal." His appeal was to the life-giving Name: "Hear me, JEHOVAH, hear me, that Thy people may know that thou art JEHOVAH their Elohim, and that

---

* Zechariah xi. 12.

thou hast turned their heart back again," *i.e.*, to the ancestral faith, based as that is upon immutable TRUTH. "And when the people saw the Divine fire consume the altar-sacrifice, they fell on their faces, exclaiming יְהֹוָה הוּא הָאֱלֹהִים JEHOVAH He is the Elohim."

In conclusion, the Rabbi expresses his fervent hope that he has succeeded in furnishing his disciples "with strong weapons to defend the citadel of"—what? Only Rabbinical Judaism; whose most formidable assailant from *without* is the direct light of the law and the testimony, which, together with other fresh elements and influences, must prove fatal to that at best negative, and now superannuated vestage of ages when Scripture, as an individual gift, was unknown. "I say to *defend*," continues the Rabbi, "for nothing could be farther from my thoughts than to *attack* the religious convictions of those who conscientiously differ from us in creed." Those who hold the all-sufficiency of the written Word, irrespective of all creeds, may well question the sincerity of the Rabbi where "the religious *convictions*" of such as differ from his creed are concerned. For it is just where these are the most earnestly and tenderly cherished, that his envenomed darts are aimed. If the Rabbi would openly attack our many glaring inconsistencies and shortcomings, &c., &c., as professing followers of a Master who taught and illustrated perfect obedience to the Father, perfect love to humankind, even to enemies, we might have some reason to thank him for thus making us feel ashamed of ourselves; but instead of this appreciation of our English forbearance under personal or national rebuke, we are wounded in the person of our best friend and benefactor. Wounded as it were in the apple of the eye—we feel intensely aggrieved, and ask, why is it that one who shares all the blessings of our free country should abuse his freedom, by failing to comprehend the generous and noble emotions that freedom should inspire, and free men exemplify?

SERMON XII.

The Twelfth Sermon begins with a passage from the prophet Isaiah (xl. 6—8): "The voice said, Proclaim. And I replied, What shall I proclaim? All flesh is grass, and all the beauty thereof as the flower of the grass. The grass withereth, the flower fadeth, for the Spirit of Jehovah bloweth upon it: surely the people is grass. The grass withereth, the flower fadeth, but the Word of our Elohim endureth for ever." In this emphatic declaration the Rabbi sees only one aspect of the subject, that of the LAW *recorded*, not that of the WORD *spoken* in another form. He should remember that the *voice* of the Divine WORD uttered, and HIS *hand* recorded His law on tables of stone.

The Rabbi continues: "'God will never alter his law, nor change it for another.' No new dispensation has ever, can ever, come to supersede or abrogate the law given from Sinai. 'For the word of our God shall stand for ever.'" The element of the Law being LOVE, of which *righteousness* is the inseparable characteristic, the change must be in the *nature* and *character* of those who, as transgressors, are *now* under its condemnation. Hence the necessity for the "new covenant" with the house of Judah and Israel. "Not according to the covenant which I made with their forefathers, which they brake. For after these days, saith JEHOVAH, I will put My Spirit within them, and write My Law in their hearts." This is assuredly the new dispensation so often alluded to, as that of the new Spirit which, when Israel is regenerated, shall supersede the broken covenant. *Hearts* no longer estranged from the WORD—the source of man's higher, nobler life—shall then be *affiliated* to the Father, and in *affinity* with His Son, the *manifester of His love*, the doer of His will, the consummator of His eternal purpose. This ministry of the Spirit shall fructify (during the Messiah's reign as Priest and King), throughout the ages to come. Hence the declaration: "I will bring you out of your graves, and I will put MY SPIRIT *within you*, and ye shall live, and I shall place you in your own land." Such is the promise of Jehovah.

"Theologians of another faith," says the Rabbi, "contend that what the prophet here predicts is the revelation of a new law by the author of their religion." ! ! If such there be they are *strays and waifs* from the faith once delivered—that which rests on immutable truth, whose testimony is, "Think not that I am come to abrogate the law or the prophets, I am come not to abolish but to fulfil." The author, exemplifier and completer of that faith was the Word embodied. Having on earth glorified the Divine law, not only by meeting in his own person its exaction (death for transgression), but during his brief personal ministry, as witness to truth, by having asserted the supremacy and all-sufficiency of the law and the testimony, superseded as these *then* were by the *burdensome additions and traditions of the Sanhedrin.* What is the one *indispensable* requirement, and how has it been accepted? "*This one thing I demanded of them*, saying, *Obey my voice,* and I will be your ELOHIM, and ye shall be my people; and walk ye in *my ways*, that I have ordained, that it may be well with you." But they hearkened not nor gave heed, but walked in the devices and stubbornness of their evil hearts, and retrograded instead of going forward. "Since the day that your fathers came forth from the land of Mizraim unto this day, I have sent to you all my servants the prophets, timely sending them, yet they hearkened not . . . but did worse than their fathers. Therefore thou shalt speak all these words to them, but *they will not hearken to thee;* thou shalt call to them, but *they will not respond.* Therefore thou shalt say, it is a nation that *obeys not the voice of* JEHOVAH *their Elohim*, nor accepteth His correction. TRUTH is ignored, it is cut off from their mouth. Is there *no* balm in Gilead, *no* physician there? Why then is the *health* of the daughter of my people *not recovered?*" Rabbinical artifice taught not only how to *evade* the direct requirements of the *Law*, but impiously superseded its authority by *rival requirements;* so that, to *this* day, "authority and authority" still contend for the mastery. Hence the complaint, "My people have been guilty of two great evils; they have forsaken Me, the fountain of living waters, and have devised for themselves cisterns, broken cisterns, that can hold no water." Jehovah, the hope of Israel, all that forsake thee shall be ashamed. It is well to know that there is now "*salt*" incorporated with the *inert* and apathetic mass, well characterized as "devotional *ignorants*," *superstitious* in mind and practice.

"How then dare Christianity assert," continues the Rabbi, "that a purer and more elevated morality than that contained in the Bible was preached by its founder? The word of God could not have been *imperfect* or *incomplete*, so as to require either correction or development." Alas, the perfect completeness of the Divine WORD has as yet been practically recognised by comparatively few, and it was this very all-sufficiency which the *embodied* WORD asserted and maintained, in face of the orthodox chief priests, scribes and pharisees, who practically ignored it. "Where the so-called 'new dispensation,'" says the Rabbi, "agrees with the Bible, it must be needless repetition." When the Divine Law, as a rule of life, *is written on the heart* (thus in accordance with the first command) it will not be a "needless repetition," but an *actuating* principle of the new, *i.e., regenerate* life.

A little sentimental ejaculation here follows, the meaning of which it is impossible to divine. "Ah, brethren, amid the fair bowers and the unshaded glory of Paradise, Adam *needed to hear his Father's voice, to keep him from sin.*"!! Does the Rabbi suppose that this voice served to do more than admonish Adam of the penalty which transgression would incur? It did not *fortify* against the tempter. We have, therefore, great cause to be thankful for the gracious promise that "the seed of the woman" shall eventually have under his heel the head of the deceiver; in other words, have power to subdue all that is hostile to the supreme will. The inspired Psalmist comments on the Divine WORD, in the recorded form, as a light in the way of wisdom, and as a lamp to our feet in the path of peace. The Rabbi has yet to be weaned from misleading *ignis fatuus.* "Study our Law," he adds, "by the *help* of the light shed upon it *by our sages and commentators*." Speed the time in which Israel shall arise and shine in the light of Jehovah's countenance, rejoicing in HIS *salvation*, awake to His behests, devoted to His will, active in His service; thus realizing the promise, "I will give them pastors after my own heart, who shall feed them with knowledge and understanding" (Jer. iii. 15), elsewhere described as "*clean*" provender,* *winnowed* with shovel and with fan (Isaiah xxx. 24).

---

* Evidently separated from orthodox and traditional defilement.

"At that time they shall call Jerusalem the Throne of JEHOVAH, and all nations shall be gathered to it, to the NAME of JEHOVAH. Neither shall they any more walk according to the devices of their evil heart, for My name shall be supreme among the Gentiles, saith Jehovah. The whole earth shall be filled with My glory." *

"Therefore wait ye upon Me, saith JEHOVAH, until the day that I rise up to the prey: for My determination is to gather the nations, that I may assemble the kingdoms, to pour upon them mine indignation, even all My fierce anger: for all the earth shall be devoured with the fire of My indignation. For then will I turn to the people a pure language, that they may all call upon the name of JEHOVAH, to serve Him with one consent. I will also leave in the midst of thee an afflicted and poor people, and they shall trust in the name of JEHOVAH. The remnant of Israel shall not do iniquity, nor speak lies; neither shall a deceitful tongue be found in their mouth: for they shall feed and rest, and none shall make them afraid. Sing, O daughter of Zion; shout, O Israel; be glad and rejoice with all thy heart, O daughter of Jerusalem. JEHOVAH hath taken away thy judgments, He hath cast out thine enemy: the King of Israel, even JEHOVAH, is in the midst of thee: thou shall not see evil any more. In that day it shall be said to Jerusalem, Fear thou not: and to Zion, Let not thine hands be slack. JEHOVAH thy Elohim in the midst of thee is mighty; He will save, He will rejoice over thee with joy; He will REST in His love, He will joy over thee with singing." (Zephaniah iii. 8—17.)

---

* Jeremiah iii. 17. Matthew xxv. 31, &c.

www.ingramcontent.com/pod-product-compliance
Lightning Source LLC
Chambersburg PA
CBHW020730100426
42735CB00038B/1523